Mom,

I hope you find these stories amusing and maybe similar to your own. Merry Christmas!

Luv, Michelle

Dec., 2000

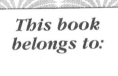

LORRAINE BLASHILL

Remembering the '50s

Growing Up In Western Canada

ORCA BOOK PUBLISHERS

Canadian Cataloguing in Publication Data
Blashill, Lorraine, 1945-
Remembering the Fifties

ISBN 1-55143-091-6
1. Canada, Western—Biography. 2. Canada, Western—Civilization. 3. Prairie Provinces—History—1945-* 4. British Columbia—History—1945-* 5. Canadians—Interviews. I. Title.
FC3219.1.B42 1997 971.2'03'0922 C97-910426-2
F1060.92.B42 1997

Library of Congress Catalog Card Number: 97-68867

Cover design by Jim Brennan
Printed and bound in Canada

Orca Book Publishers   Orca Book Publishers
PO Box 5626, Station B   PO Box 468
Victoria, BC   V8R 6S4   Custer, WA 98240-0468
Canada   USA

97 98 99 5 4 3 2 1

With love to Cory

This is how it was
back in our good old days

▷ Acknowledgements

Thanks to my sister Audrey who shared her memories and photographs and who gave me many valuable contacts. Thanks also to Susan and Harvey Cobler of Saskatoon for loaning me their collection of fifties magazines and Betty and Bob Bruce who allowed us to photograph fifties artifacts in their store, Elizabeth's Art and Collectibles, in Chemainus, BC. I'm grateful to Gary Madden who showed us through his collection of records and jukeboxes. I appreciate the enthusiasm and expertise of the group at Orca Book Publishers, especially Bob, Christine, Susan and Andrew. My thanks also to Peter, my best friend and husband, for his usual excellent photographic work and for continual enthusiasm and encouragement. Most importantly to everyone who took the time to remember—thanks for the memories.

▷ Introduction

In April 1995, I celebrated my fiftieth birthday. A month later I was retired, my job gone due to down-sizing. Having grown up in western Canada in the 1950s, this turn of events had not been part of my life plan, at least not at this stage. I expected, as most of my generation did, to work to retirement at a respectable age—sixty or sixty-five years old. When I was a child, I understood that people worked throughout their adult lives and that finding and keeping employment was a given. In my experience, jobs had always been plentiful. When I was growing up in the fifties, the average unemployment rate was 2.9 percent. For the most part, men and women of my generation have known little of unemployment. Some dropped out of school confident that jobs—good jobs—would be available. And they were.

On the other hand, our parents had endured the hardships of the 1930s. Many had served their country during the Second World War and all had been affected by it. They took nothing for granted. As children in the fifties, we took everything for granted. We had not been tested as our parents had.

We remember our childhood free of the concerns of the larger world. Our world was our neighbourhood, our community—a familiar and unthreatening place, while every other place in the world was remote and undefined. We remember a time when we could play and feel safe in doing so, out-of-sight of parents or other adults. For many of us, extended family lived nearby so we had an innate sense of our place in life and of the continuance and permanence of the family unit. It seemed obvious then to accept the lessons that our parents taught us about respect for others, especially our elders and those in authority. Teachers, ministers and political figures were all considered inviolate symbols of what was "right." The companies where our parents worked and the social, cultural and religious organizations they belonged to were, for the most part, paternalistic dictatorships. Father knew best.

As children we knew that there were always consequences for breaking the rules. Discipline was the rule, forbearance the exception. We all remember the school strap, whether we had felt its sting or not. Its existence alone spoke volumes and we listened. Statistics show that juvenile delinquency dropped after the Second World War and remained low into the mid-fifties.

We lived with strong sexual prohibitions. Sex outside the bounds of marriage was not only frowned upon but often punished, subtly or overtly. If the rules were broken and a pregnancy outside marriage resulted, a quick wedding was often the solution to avoid the whispered condemnation of the community. In other cases, teenage girls were sent away from their families and, once having given birth, were compelled, or elected, to turn their babies over to adoptive parents.

Be good and work hard, we were told. We lived secure in the knowledge that someone was in charge—that life would unfold as it should if we just diligently applied ourselves to the task at hand and, above all, followed the rules. In most instances, we found this to be true.

There were hazards, of course. And we were not immune. The polio epidemic in 1953 hit Manitoba's children and young adults the hardest. Of the over 8,700 documented cases in Canada, 2,300 of them were reported in Manitoba. As children, we knew of the threat of polio, just as we were aware that we could and did contract other communicable diseases like measles, mumps, chicken pox and whooping cough. But like children anywhere at anytime, we did not feel particularly vulnerable. Polio was something that happened to other people. But too often it did strike—in our neighbourhood, next door, in our own home. It extracted a terrible price, leaving withered limbs and devastated bodies. Fortunate were those who escaped its grip and those who were treated at the first sign of its symptoms.

Some children suffered abuse at the hands of their parents and others in positions of authority, and most cases went unreported as children had little or no voice in this world of unquestioned parental authority. Other children faced discrimination or abuse due to their racial origin or religion or because of a physical or mental disability. The awareness that spawned social programs to redress these problems was yet to come.

Then our world began to change. Where once farming and ranching had sustained the Prairie provinces and logging and fishing were the cornerstones of economic existence in British Columbia, resource exploitation soon transformed the face of the western economy. No event was more significant to the changing fortunes of the West than the discovery of oil at Leduc, Alberta, in 1947. In the first seven years of the oil boom, an estimated $6 billion in new investment fuelled the western economy. Further resource exploitation of uranium, potash and other minerals, the building of hydro-electric dams and bumper crops in 1951 through 1953 added to the increase in wealth generation in the West.

It was not long before governments afforded the extension of electrical power to the far-flung areas of the western provinces—and life for all of us changed forever. Not only did electricity make a less labour-intensive lifestyle possible, it generated a consumer-driven retail expansion as our parents clamoured for the electrical appliances that would make their lives, and ours, easier. Soon we all had electrical stoves and refrigerators, irons and toasters, floor polishers and can openers in our homes.

The extension of electrical power came at the same time that infant television was taking its first steps. We eagerly held its hand while it grew to maturity because it brought the world to us as nothing else had. It was then that western Canada, through improved communication and transportation, and economic prosperity, became an integral part of the nation that, since Confederation, had only been possible in a limited way.

As pivotal as the times were in modern history, we took even these remarkable changes for granted. As children of the fifties, we knew no other life. The harsh lessons our parents learned during the 1930s and the war years were second-hand stories to us and seemed increasingly unreal and irrelevant as prosperity and technology changed our world. Our behaviour and beliefs from babyhood had been shaped and sharpened by family tradition and teaching. Now the growing economy and changing environment that included television and improved transportation and communication also influenced our behaviours and beliefs—and our way of life.

Technological advances increasingly mechanized farming, ranching and resource extraction. The evolving machines of the fifties gave us mobility which widened our horizons and raised our expectations. Rural living no longer required the human resources once needed to sustain it, so we left the farms and villages we grew up in and moved to the cities—cities that were growing not only from the exodus of young people from rural communities but also from immigration from eastern Canada and from other countries. Most of our parents afforded us educational opportunities they had not had. We took on a world that was increasingly unlike anything we had known in our childhood, and accustomed to change, we continually adapted. Change had become a constant factor in our lives.

In reality, it was no surprise to me as a member of the fifties generation, that in taking the step over the threshold of fifty, I found more and greater change on the other side. Part of my adapting to this change was to talk to my contemporaries—people who grew up in western Canada in the 1950s as I did. I interviewed friends and relatives and their friends and relatives. I asked for names of fifties folk at every opportunity and contacted the people suggested. Through letters to the editor in a number of western Canadian newspapers, I heard from many more.

In talking to these people of the fifties generation, I learned that they have experienced the same changes since childhood that I have, and most wonder, as I do, what changes are ahead. Some, like me, have had to adjust career plans and find different employment while others operate their own businesses. Only a few have worked with the same company throughout their careers and expect to retire from it.

In the following pages, you'll read the experiences of these people, starting with Peter P. who was born in 1935 and was a teenager in the early fifties through to Bill who was born in 1954 and was therefore a young child at the end of the 1950s—all of them part of the fifties generation. They grew up in the West from Manitoba to British Columbia and in the Yukon; in villages, in towns, in cities and on farms and ranches. Their parents worked in a wide spectrum of occupations; among them are labourers, railroad workers, teachers, business owners, salespeople, secretaries, farmers, shopkeepers and store owners, a miner, a chartered accountant, a writer, a doctor, a nurse and a rancher. Each of these fifties kids tells of their life in the fifties as they lived it. In the final chapter, they talk about what the fifties taught them and why and how things have changed so much, so quickly.

Honour thy father, but ask thy mother

Family was the centre of our lives in the fifties. We had relatively few other influences. We remember the special occasions. For some of us, it was the rare and therefore memorable trips we took with our families; for others, the day electricity arrived in our home; and for most of us, the first day we had television in our living room. We remember our day-to-day existence mostly in comparative terms. It was a different era, an uncomplicated time of conformity when we seemed to instinctively know and accept our place in life.

In the early fifties, newspapers in western Canada carried an ad that exemplified the accepted thinking of the time about family life. The ad was for nerve food, a remedy to gain relief from the stresses of life. The copy stated that Mom stayed at home and had "meals to get and dishes to wash; laundry to do and a house to clean." Dad, on the other hand, had a noisy office with machines breaking down and with all that, he had to contend with "the kitchen tap's leaking; the coal bin's low; the youngster needs glasses and the car needs repair."

We children of the fifties recognize this stereotypical presentation because it was a common portrayal of family life. We saw it not only in newspaper ads but in magazines, in picture shows and on television sitcoms. But we looked at our own families and tried to find similarities. There were few. Our parents' roles in the family were rarely as clearly defined and separate as the stereotype suggested. Some of our moms worked in stores and businesses, and on farms and ranches; some were teachers and others, nurses. Women's work in the home was labour-intensive and often done without the benefit of electricity and running water. Most often Mom was the primary parent dispensing discipline, applying home remedies for various illnesses and keeping the family organized, but she also often worked outside the home or at her kitchen table doing the books for her husband's business. We respected our fathers, of course, and sometimes feared them. After all, Dad was the majority wage earner for the family and titular head of the household which, in most cases, meant he had ultimate discipline rights.

If the popular media did not truly reflect the reality of our families, what was it really like? Each of us remembers different things—and some of the same things but in different ways.

▷ **Peter P., born in 1935**
  grew up on a farm near Winlaw in southern British Columbia

I grew up on a little farm in a community about thirty miles north of

Nelson, near Winlaw where we got our mail. Mostly the people worked in milling or logging and some farming. Some mining I guess. I was the youngest and there was my older brother and my sister was married when I was fairly young, so I grew up mostly with my brother. He was about five years older. My dad passed away in 1944 and I did have a step-dad but he passed away so I sort of grew up on my own, more or less.

We had horses on the farm for ploughing, putting in and mowing hay. That ended about the sixties. At least for me. I bought a tractor. I got tired of trying to catch the horse—easier to catch a tractor.

There was no telephone until after the power came in. Electricity didn't come there until about 1957 so we had gas lamps and coal oil lamps. We had an outdoor toilet. We did have water coming into the house—gravity water—most of the people did because there was lots of water around that area. We could have had indoor toilets, but we didn't. At that time they thought having a toilet in the house was very unsanitary. Closer to the sixties some people started putting them in and pretty soon everybody else had one.

▷ **Jim, born in 1937**
  grew up in Pipestone, Manitoba

I was born in Mitchell, Ontario. We migrated to Manitoba when I was eight months old. My mother was originally from Manitoba and they decided to move west because there was no work in Ontario. My dad was oiling on the dragline. I have a younger brother and two younger sisters, one who was born postwar.

My dad was overseas for four years during the war. There were no hired men at that time because they were all in the army. My mother worked on my grandfather's farm as a hired hand driving the tractor.

We didn't see much of my father's parents. My dad's father was a mean old man. When my dad was a kid he saved up his money and bought himself a pair of ice skates. And the old fella got hold of them, took them out and chopped them up with an axe. No kid of his was going to waste his time skating. This had a real effect on my dad and carried over into his adult life. He wouldn't do those kinds of things. He was pretty laid back, much like his mother really. She was the salt of the earth.

I saw my grandparents on my mother's side a lot. They had a farm three miles out of town. I pretty much lived there. Every Friday night

Jim and his family, circa 1952. Jim stands third from the left.

I'd phone them up and ask if I could come out for the weekend. The answer was always yes and I'd hitch a ride with the guy who ran the mail route, the rural delivery. At about eight o'clock Saturday morning, I'd go down to the post office and ask him if I could get a ride to my grandma's place and he would say sure and away we'd go. He'd dump me off at the gate. Sometimes I'd stay the whole weekend and he'd pick me up on the run on Monday morning into town. I spent a lot of time out there. Went swimming, riding horseback.

▷ **Elaine, born in 1938**
grew up in the village of Botha, Alberta

I grew up in Botha near Stettler. I have a sister five years younger and a brother ten years younger. I remember we'd bathe every Sunday morning. It was a ritual. The tub would be hauled in from the porch and warm water put in. The baby would be bathed first, then more hot water would be added and the next one would bathe and so on.

My grandpa and grandma on my mom's side lived about two miles out of town. My grandma on my dad's side lived in town. You did things for them. My grandma on my dad's side had broke her hip and lived alone so I would go and sleep at her place often to make sure she was okay. Then once a week probably, in junior high, I always went out and stayed overnight at Grandpa and Grandma's. It was kind of a ritual. I got spoiled.

Elaine, fifteen years old in 1953.

Mom taught music and I always made supper from the time I was a little girl. Probably around twelve or so. I don't know that it was something I had to do but it was something I liked to do and I just went ahead and did it.

I can remember once us getting mad at Mom and saying, "Okay, we're going to live in our bedroom." So we took a hot plate in there. That would last from Saturday night until she made a really good dinner on Sunday!

Every Sunday morning we put buckets on the handlebars of our bikes and rode to the ice rink. We would fill them with water and carry them back home so Mom could heat it the next morning to wash clothes. Mom would be done by noon and we'd haul the wash water out. It didn't hurt us a darn bit. Later we had a well close to the house but we never did have running water when I was home. Now if we have something on for ten minutes, it goes in the wash! It sure wasn't like that then.

▷ **Gary, born in 1938 in Manitoba**
 grew up in Vancouver, British Columbia

My mom worked at Woodward's as a cashier in the stationery department. It's amazing what a mother could do in those days. Running those old washing machines, starching and ironing shirts and cooking meals. She had Wednesday and Sunday off from Woodward's.

We had a wall phone and at that time we were on a party line. You'd dial the exchange. We were out in the Alma exchange. There was also a Fairmont exchange. You'd dial the first two letters and then the number.

For home remedies we had mustard plasters to layer on our chests and Vicks to sniff and, of course, Buckley's cough medicine. I remember that! I don't know if the mustard plasters did you any good but they made your chest awful red.

▷ **Dwayne, born in 1939**
grew up in Brandon, Manitoba

I was born on a farm just outside of Benito, Manitoba, and we moved to Brandon when I was only one. My dad became a farm machinery dealer so I was brought up in the city but I still had family ties back up in Benito. I was an only child.

Dad actually started the business on his farm just outside of Benito. He sold five tractors, I believe, in 1939. That was almost unheard of in that district. So they came to him at the end of '39 and told him that they'd lost their dealer and there was an opening in Brandon. That was the Minneapolis Moline farm machinery company. So they asked him to open up a dealership here and so he scraped and scrounged and all the rest of it, and sold off some land and came down and started up the implement business.

My mother was not always that well. She found it a little hard to manage so it was nice for her to get me out of the house. I spent a lot of time with my dad at the machinery business. It was a good way for the two of us to be out from underfoot. We had a maid to look after the house, to help with the home chores. It wasn't that Mom couldn't walk around but she just wasn't well enough to do a lot of things.

I had polio in 1948 when I was nine. And I got it on the last half-day of school. We were just supposed to show up to get our report cards and I didn't get my report card. I think my dad had to drive around and get it for me. I was sleeping on the verandah, a very hot morning, and when I woke up I had an extremely sore throat, a severe headache and so on. About half an hour after I woke up, I went into convulsions. There was a nurse next door who was a friend of ours and when I started convulsing, my mother phoned her and she came over and immediately knew what was going on. There was a lot of polio around at that particular point and lots of kids in the area were being struck down. They called the ambulance, took me to the hospital and immediately started giving me penicillin. That was probably the first year in Brandon that they were giving the kids penicillin. It seemed to be working quite well. I was in the hospital for a week. Because I was rushed to hospital and given penicillin early enough, it broke the fever within the first three days. If you could do that with polio, you'd won the game. There were kids out on farms, twenty or thirty miles out of town, and they wouldn't be brought in until the following day. They would end up in an iron lung for sure. There was about six schools in Brandon so you would always hear that two or three students from one school or another had contracted polio and some ended up in an iron lung. I think to myself, Am I ever lucky.

I was told when I came out of the hospital that I had to go to the Kiwanis swimming pool here in town where I was to get my only exercises. I was not to ride my bike. I was not to walk upright for the first two weeks after I was out of hospital. I was just to sit in a chair or move around on my knees. I didn't follow all their instructions though. When my mother wasn't watching, I would be up walking around or out riding my bike.

I was just reading about how some of the symptoms of polio seem to be returning. Some of the symptoms these people have reported recurring are respiratory problems which they associate with polio. Although the polio I had was in my hips and my knees, I have had a few lung problems and lots of aches and pains in my legs. I, just like everybody else, thought, Well, it's just old age coming on. Now I'm beginning to wonder if maybe it has to do with polio. I didn't think too much about it at the time but I think about it more today. At that time it was just one of those things you'd rather forget—something like having measles. I had measles about five times—and it's something you'd like to forget.

▷ **Marilyn, born in 1940**
grew up at Lake Cowichan, British Columbia

My father ran the local grocery store. My mother was a stay-at-home mom who did what women so often do—the books that were associated with a small business. I grew up in a lumbering and logging community. The resource-based industries tended to hire mainly men. It was heavy work and was done by men, and the women stayed at home. In later years my mom and dad started a newspaper in Lake Cowichan—or at least my dad started it and then my mom had to do it. As I look back, I realize Dad had wonderful ideas and Mother had to follow up with the work associated with them.

When I was thirteen in 1953, my baby sister was born. That would have had an impact on the reason for my mom being at home. In the late fifties, when that child began kindergarten I was just leaving home, and Mom was out in the workforce.

The author as a telephone operator, her summer job in 1962.

In about 1952 we moved out of town and built a house. We didn't have electricity or a telephone. My dad eventually hooked up a generator but before that we had kerosene lamps, a gas refrigerator, a gas iron and Mom had a gas washer-dryer all in one so the clothes went into the same hole to be washed and to be dried. That was the very first washer we had seen. Up until then she had had a wringer. And we had a chemical toilet. But my mom or somebody didn't know how to work the chemical toilet and actually used the sawdust that was packing the chemical, thinking that was what we were supposed to use as the chemical to break down the debris. That didn't work very well.

In those days our primary fuel was sawdust. I remember having a sawdust hopper on our stove and having to fill up the sawdust buckets outside. I can also remember one time putting chewing gum down the sawdust hopper. You could get rid of a gum wrapper or other paper in the sawdust hopper because it would go down with the sawdust and burn when it got into the fire at the bottom. The gum, however, caused the sawdust to get kind of sticky and it wouldn't flow like it should and the fire would go out. Not a smooth move!

We eventually got a generator and hooked up lights in the house. That was an amazing moment. I can remember being out on a date and driving back onto the property and the lights all were on. That was really an exciting moment.

When we got a telephone in about 1954, we were on a party line with five or six other people. Our telephone number was 2-4Y. When the telephone rang one long and two short rings, it was for us, whereas other people were two longs or three shorts or some other combination. Of course, the local telephone operator knew everything about everybody because she was the one who pushed the plug in to connect lines. We were always amazed at how she knew everything that was going on in the community.

▷ **Audrey H., born in 1941**
  grew up on a farm near Strongfield in south-central Saskatchewan

We were on a telephone party line so our business was everybody's business. A long ring on the line meant that everyone was to listen and it was usually an announcement about a fowl supper, bazaar, funeral or some happening that involved the whole community. The long ring also announced emergencies, like fires, so everyone could rush out and help. The telephone office had regular working hours, so after 10:00 pm one could not make a long distance call. Summer hours were longer to accommodate the farming community.

Wall phone typical of those on farms in the West throughout the fifties.

Travelling salesmen were still common in the fifties, selling everything from horse liniment to aluminum pots and pans. I remember the Watkins' and the Rawleigh salesmen in particular.

▷ **Maxine, born in 1942**
  grew up in Gypsumville, Manitoba

I grew up in Gypsumville, Manitoba, between Lake Manitoba and Lake Winnipeg, about a hundred and seventy miles north of Winnipeg. I lived in the village which served the surrounding farming community. The land up there is really bush country and not really suitable for farming. The majority of the farmers were immigrants who came from the farms in the Ukraine and Poland. That's what they knew how to do so that's what they did.

I come from a large family and have two brothers and four sisters; I'm the second and the oldest girl. Because we were essentially a family of girls, we all had to split wood, carry water and do other tasks usually reserved for boys in those days.

My mother and father were probably among the best-educated parents in town. If you took them out of the equation, the highest education would have probably been grade three or so. Most of the villagers were barely literate. My mother went to that part of the country to teach and my father ran the post office and the general store in the village. That's how they met. My father fought in the First World War and when he came back from overseas, he went up there with his father and a crew to survey a railway line. He ended up staying and buying out the general store that was there at the time.

Dad was definitely the head of the household and life was really quite structured. We didn't have much outside information. We got power when I was about ten, I think. So we had no power and no running water for most of my younger years. So that meant we largely spent time doing real things. We had to go to CGIT (Canadian Girls in Training) and Explorers, then there was choir practice starting when we were seven or eight.

▷ **Peter B., born in 1942 in England**
came to Canada in 1944 and grew up in Regina, Saskatchewan

My dad was a Canadian soldier and he married my mom in England. Mom and I came to Canada on a troop ship, landing in New York in 1944. She tells the story of how the ship was blacked out at night in order to avoid enemy planes and ships and how the captain ordered the mothers to give their little ones beer at night to keep them quiet. She was an English war bride, having married a man who was the youngest in a large family and certainly his mother's favourite child. Consequently, Mom met with some hostility from his family and had to adapt and manage largely on her own. She worked cleaning other peoples' homes for most of my growing-up years. Mom was raised in an orphanage of some kind so was ill-equipped to cope with kids and a home, although she no doubt did the best she could. When Dad came back from the war, he was "shell-shocked," that's what they called it then. Today they'd probably call it post-traumatic stress syndrome. He was a troubled man for the rest of his life.

We lived near Regina Avenue and Elphinstone, a lowland where the ball parks are now. Wascana Creek always flooded over in the spring and Dad would have to take a rowboat to go to work. He worked at a lumber company and later for the railroad.

We didn't have indoor plumbing so we made do with an outhouse which was regularly visited by the man with the "honey wagon," pulled by a horse. We also had ice delivered by horse and wagon. There were wooden sidewalks parallel to deep ditches. I remember once riding my tricycle along the sidewalk and going over the side into the ditch. It was a mishap that almost cost me my manhood!

My mother, being Catholic, raised me as a Catholic, hoping, I think, that I would be a priest one day. So I served my time as an altar boy. One day a couple of us altar boys got into the priest's wine and discovered a new feeling!

It was about then that I noticed how poor people, including my parents, would give their last dollar to the church. In later years, after remembering the big car the priest drove, I resented the church for taking so callously from the poor—which included my family. Needless to say, I didn't become a priest.

I remember happy times, like Christmas. My favourite gift was a stuffed rocking horse.

After one of the spring floods, my father found the basement full of rats. Over the winter I'd collected a number of stray cats, a practice my mother frowned upon. The rats had to be dealt with so my father threw all of my cats into the basement. When it was all over, three cats were dead, others were scarred. But all the rats were gone. I was horrified.

▷ **Bob, born in 1943**
grew up in Regina, Saskatchewan

Dad worked for the railroad until he retired. Mother was the main disciplinarian because Dad worked shifts and she never worked outside the home. I refuse to say she never worked because she worked tremendously hard. I can recall times when she tried to help out by taking in sewing and doing that sort of thing but with the size of family that she had there was just too much to do. Of course, when I came along in 1943 she had a pretty good crop of built-in baby-sitters; my sister was seven, a brother was eight, another ten, and my older brother was sixteen or seventeen years of age.

When I was born things were starting to improve a bit, and of course within a year or so the war was over and the economy picked up. I came along at a time when the financial situation within the household was changing dramatically. I was able to benefit substantially from being the baby in the family. I got to do a lot of things and I was given a lot more material things.

I can remember getting up in the mornings to go to school. Mother was always the first one up at maybe half past five or six o'clock in the morning. She continued that for years, even after Dad retired and all of us were gone. She would get up, go down to the basement and get the big coal-fired furnace going. Then she'd come upstairs where she would fire up the coal stove in the kitchen. She'd get all the long underwear for the boys and she would take it down and put it over the door of the oven. Then she'd come and wake us up. And we had warm longjohns to put on.

I remember the rule was I was in bed at seven o'clock at night. Yes, on a school night I was in bed at seven o'clock! I don't think there's anything harder on a kid than going to bed early on a summer evening. And summer evenings on the prairies are late anyway. Being in bed at that time of night was tough with all the other kids in the neighbourhood out playing, even the kids that were my age. Mother always said, "You've got school in the morning." I never suffered because of it. It just seemed tough at the time.

▷ **John, born in 1943**
  grew up in Winnipeg, Manitoba

I was born at a very early age. That kind of sets the scene! I was the middle child. There were two older and two younger—the oldest a sister and then an older brother, then two younger sisters.

At that time, extended family lived all around you. My grandmother on my mother's side lived right next door for awhile. When my dad built a new house she moved two doors over. My dad's mother lived about five houses down the street and there were aunts and uncles and cousins. At one point when I was older, my grandmother became sick and we had a buzzer set up with a wire that went to her house so if she needed help she could press the buzzer. My dad later built an addition to the house and his mother came and lived at our house. So there was kind of a sense of family and responsibility happening at the same time.

We lived in a part of Winnipeg called North Kildonan. We had an outhouse out back and we'd go down the street to get water at the water pipe. The neighbourhood was made up of a lot of Mennonites who had pioneered that particular part of Winnipeg. My mother has a picture of herself standing in front of her house that at one time was used as a chicken coop or something. The Mennonites built the church and really took care of each other. There was definitely a sense of community. The negative side of this was that there were Mennonites and then there was the English—us and them. When you're a kid you feel protected but there was also a barrier to keep people out. You could always tell, and you can to this day, the people with a Mennonite background—by their names. There were always ways of knowing where the line was drawn. In the neighbourhood you would know people for blocks and could go down the street and you would name people in this block and that block. Now you might know one or two of your neighbours.

One of my childhood memories is the way my dad smelled when he came home from work. And I'll bet that most people remember what their dad smelled like. My dad worked in a tannery so it was a leathery, chemical smell. I remember that distinctly.

As for discipline, my brother was a rebel and he used to get a spanking every Saturday—that was a regular thing. And it was from Dad. He was head of the family, although in looking back my mother probably had a whole lot more influence than I realized. My dad has passed away but my mother is still alive. She's a very strong person and is capable of surviving a whole lot better than he would have been. In some ways she was probably the real strength in the family. But at that time the order of things was that Dad was head of the family. On Saturday we had to clean out the basement or work in the garden or something. My brother didn't like doing chores so watching him get spanked was enough to keep me doing the right things.

One of my grandmothers lived down the street and she used to have parties for us grandkids. She used to give us Pepsi and hot dogs. My other grandmother also lived close by—she liked to spoil me. I'd go over there after school and she would give me something to eat. She'd put icing on stuff. That was kind of nice. A single lady down the street was the aunt of somebody I knew—every year she would have a Valentine's party for a bunch of kids. That was an annual event for us.

My dad was a deacon of the church so he'd visit sick people. I remember him taking a sack of potatoes or groceries to a widow. People helping people was very important.

Saturday night was bath night and we bathed in a tin tub. I don't know how often the water was changed or if it was changed at all—but there was five kids and two adults.

One of the reasons I have bad hearing is because I had a punctured ear drum that came from having an ear infection. Nowadays, if a kid had an infection, you'd do something. But in those days, a doctor wasn't called unless it got really serious. I think my infection could have been prevented if I had gone to a doctor. When I was a baby, I almost died of malnutrition because my mother's milk wasn't good or something and when I was in grade eleven I had acute appendicitis. Dentists were for when the pain started and not for keeping teeth clean. You often ended up having teeth pulled. He used to put water in the hypodermic I think—at least that's how it felt! There was no alcohol in the house but there was a medicine called Alpenkreuter. It was a medicine for adults— I don't think my parents had it but my grandparents did—they took this stuff for minor illnesses. It had alcohol in it. Maybe some adults got more colds than they needed too!

In the summer we used to go to my uncle's farm who lived near Killarney, Manitoba, a four-hour trip. It would be standard to fix a flat on the car somewhere on the way. They lived without electricity and had kerosene lamps. We were big city folk compared to them!

▷ **Lil, born in 1944**
grew up in and near Nampa in northern Alberta

My dad built a small cafe in Nampa in the fall of 1947 with living quarters upstairs. The oil boom was on. The hours were long for both my mom and my dad as the cafe was open from 6:00 a.m. to midnight. Sometimes if there was a dance in the community hall, which was quite a frequent event in those days, they would stay open all night. It was tough without power or water. They would haul water from the river during the summer and melt snow in the winter months. There were gas lamps, which of course had to be kept full and pumped, in the kitchen area and another in the eating area. Ham and eggs with hashbrowns, dessert and all the coffee you could drink cost a dollar. Pie and coffee was thirty-five cents. When I look back through the pictures (I was three years old, Lorraine four and Roseanne five years old), it never ceases to amaze me that with all the work that had to be done, my mom always found the time in her busy schedule to keep three young girls in ringlets all the time.

During this period Dad was also farming. Lots of times Dad would take us three girls out to the farm to give Mom a break from us underfoot all the time. In 1949, Dad built a small twelve-volt generator for lights. That really helped in the cafe.

My kittens were my playmates for hours at a time. I remember one afternoon when Mom was busy, my sister took my kittens away from me and ran upstairs. Naturally I tattled to Mom who in turn called my sister to give them back immediately, which she did. She threw them at me from the top of the stairs. I still have faint scars on my face and have a real dislike for cats to this day.

In 1951, I was seven and Dad leased out the cafe in exchange for machinery and we moved back out to the farm. We lived in two granaries. One served as a kitchen, the other as a bedroom. We always had a huge garden to tend to, water to haul, chickens to feed and roots to pick. Dad went to work as a Cat operator and cut brush for farmers in the district. His wages were a dollar an hour, three times more than the railroad paid.

We had a small Massey tractor that Mom used for everything, from going to Nampa, shopping for groceries, to taking us to church and going with Father to visit Memere and Papere. We went to school that winter by cutter. It was equipped with a little stove and lots of blankets. Mom would bundle us up and always check to make sure we were all wearing our thick brown stockings and bloomers.

In 1952 Mom and Dad sold the cafe and Dad built an eighteen-by-thirty-two-foot house in Nampa. Baba and Gedo lived just through the trees behind us. Dad had some heifers fenced up behind the house that had to be taken to graze and we took turns doing that. Friends would come out and help. We rode Gedo's goats when he wasn't around. We teased them and received head butts in return. Once we took them up the annex on the elevator for walks to see if they would fall, to see how sure-footed they actually were. Meanwhile, the heifers got away so I tied up Gedo's favourite kid and, as we went to chase the cows back into the unfenced area, forgot all about it. Gedo found it hanging dead the next morning. He excluded me from all he did with the kids that summer. He would spend hours with them, building houses in the bush out of interwoven branches and willows. Completely ignoring me. That was enough already! I'm sorry, give me a good licking with a willow—anything! Just get it over. But he never did.

Dad worked for Midland Pacific Grain Elevators (later it became United Grain Growers). By this time Dad had bought land. His home section was 320 acres of solid bush and he had 90 acres of that brush cut and piled. As the song went, "I'm not a root picker not a root picker's son, but I'll pick roots 'til the root pickin's done." And damn, I did. I picked roots for years and year. So did my sisters. By the time my brother was old enough to pick roots, the roots were all picked. Dad paid us a certain amount a pile but he'd also tan my hide if I stuffed the pile with trees from the surrounding just so I could beat Dona (a man Dad hired) with more and larger piles. I had an advantage because whenever Dona was paid, he'd disappear for a few days and when he eventually showed up to work I would have been busily picking. My dad would not allow us to pick roots alone because of the bears. You could see them from time to time but they usually were as afraid of you as you were of them.

We moved across the street into a new United Grain Growers' house. This house not only had electric lights, it had running water also. Still no usable bathroom as the town did not have a sewer system. These were great times, living in town, going to school, working on the farm after school, riding bikes, picnics and playing ball. Mom worked at the cafe then so I had to look after my little brother. I got to be very good with time. Mom and Dad would go out curling or to play cards and five-or-so minutes after they left, I'd have Stan dressed in his snowsuit, skates over my back and we would be off to the school rink. I always got home just before Mom and Dad. Once, rushing in the front door as their car was pulling in the backyard, I had to flip Stan into bed, snowsuit and all. My heart was beating so loudly I was certain the neighbours could hear it. Later, I sneaked in to put him into his pajamas. He was a wonderful secret-keeper.

▷ **Linda H., born in 1944**
  grew up on a farm near Marsden, Saskatchewan

My mom came from a big family and so there were always lots of people around, lots of kids. We had a big house. My mother was the oldest in her family so they all seemed to come to her, to our house.

My dad played violin and he used to play for dances on Saturday nights. We'd all pile in the car and go wherever he was playing. I remember being younger and falling asleep on school benches.

I remember the old gas lamps before we had power. Between the time I was eleven and twelve years old, we got our own generator so we were considered very rich. We got power not long after. My father died when I was thirteen and my mother didn't even know how to fill out a cheque or know what they had in the way of money. It was very traumatic for her. My older sister and her husband came and took over the farm so that worked out well.

We had a '56 Buick. It was such a wonderful car. Mother drove, which was rare at the time. She put one vehicle through the end of the garage by stepping on the gas instead of the brake. And I remember us kids just roaring, killing ourselves laughing, and she got out of the car crying and we realized that it was not that funny after all.

▷ **JoAnne, born in 1944**
grew up in Dawson City, Yukon

I have an older brother, a younger brother and two even-younger sisters. One of my sisters was born in 1951 and the other in 1958. In the late forties in Dawson City, we didn't have a highway or any kind of road out. Everything that we had came in on river steamers. I remember running down to the docks to watch the boats come in with all our supplies. It was a big event when the first boat came in the spring and was always kind of a sad day when the last one left in the fall, in early October, or even late September. After that we wouldn't have any way of getting anything until the following spring when the ice melted in late April or the first part of May. Sometimes it would be late May, early June before the steamer came in. A plane brought the mail. Things were very expensive then.

My grandfather, on my mother's side, came up here shortly after the gold rush. He worked for the city. At one time he ran a bakery and did other things like that. My father came to Dawson City in 1935 from the Okanagan. He went to work for the big mining company that was there at the time, Consolidated Gold Corporation. That's where he met my mother who was working as a secretary in the office. My mother was born and raised in Dawson and had gone to school there before going to Vancouver to Sprott-Shaw College, before returning to Dawson. They married in 1938, left Consolidated Gold Corporation and bought Winaut's General Store in 1942 and operated it until the 1970s. In the first building the store was on the main floor and our living quarters were upstairs. Then my father had a new building built in the early fifties with the store in the front and the living quarters in the back.

During the late forties, my father had a bicycle. As there were three

The Winaut store in Dawson City which was also the family residence. JoAnne and her older brother stand on the sidewalk in front of her younger brother on the street, circa 1952.

of us children, one sat on a seat on the back of the bicycle, one on the frame bar and one on the handlebars. This was our means of transportation. In 1949 he was able to order a vehicle, a GMC panel van. The only way for the vehicle to get to Dawson was on a barge pulled behind a river boat. The vehicle did not get on the last boat in the fall so my father had the use of a 1948 pickup for the winter. When the first river boat arrived in the spring, on board was our new 1949 vehicle. This was very thrilling, everyone was there and we were all so excited. My family still has this vehicle.

The next and only other vehicle my father ever owned was a 1956 Pontiac. By this time there was a road between Dawson City and Whitehorse, so my parents caught a ride to Whitehorse with friends and returned with the new car. This was also another very exciting event. Everyone in town was talking about this new red and white car. We still have that one too.

My mom had all the home remedies. Like mustard plasters. Some of them were pretty hot stuff and I think they just about killed us! I still rub Vicks on my chest if I have a sore throat and put the old rag around the neck. And I gargle with salt and water. I remember my mother's poultices, but I don't know what she put in them.

Although a lot of women did not work outside the home, many of the women who lived downtown did work. They were in business of one sort of another with their husbands. It was necessary for these women to take care of the home and help manage the businesses. Some of them would hire high school students to help with the housework and look after the children.

I remember the floods. There would have been maybe five hundred people in Dawson City at that time. Everybody would be out filling sandbags, pitching in, worried about the town. They'd call the whole school out to come and fill sandbags. We had fun trying to save our town.

I remember a few tragic fires. There was a Northern Commercial Store that burned in December 1951, and I remember standing on our back porch watching that. There weren't that many stores in Dawson City so, as a result of that, my parents' store got so busy because it was one of the few left to shop at. We were open until eleven o'clock at night just trying to keep up to the demand. It was a general store. We had ladies', men's and children's wear, books, materials, threads, that sort of thing. But no groceries. My father used to say, "Nothing to eat, smoke, drink or chew."

The hospital burned down and some died in that fire. And then the school burned. These fires always seemed to happen in the winter. With the added problem of low water pressure it was almost impossible to save a building once the fire took hold.

My family lived right downtown in the business part of the community. There was a house of ill repute just down the block from us that was still operating until the early sixties. Children were welcome at this house and sometimes kids would go there after school and were given cookies and pop. The madam who operated the house was always considered to be very much a lady and was a respected member of the community, by the majority. Eventually a few people who did not approve of her or her activities had the authorities put her out of business.

There were a lot of natives in the community. And whites and there were some Japanese. Although there didn't seem to be prejudice to any great extent, when we went to church the natives were on one side and the whites on the other. I'm not sure why that was, but that always bothered me. That's the way it was.

▷ **Dennice, born in 1944**
grew up on a farm near Dodsland, Saskatchewan

I grew up on a farm. All I remember from before I went to school was my mom and dad being hailed out and rusted out and the fields being overrun with grasshoppers. My mother went back to teaching school.

One of the things I remember most about growing up on the prairies is the sound of summer. On a hot summer day there'd be a buzz in the air, I guess from all the bugs. Another memory is the screen door slamming. I think that every child who grew up on the prairies remembers their mother saying, "Shut the door." The screen door was to keep the flies out of the house and it always slammed because they had spring-loaded catches and they'd wear out and the door would slam when you shut it.

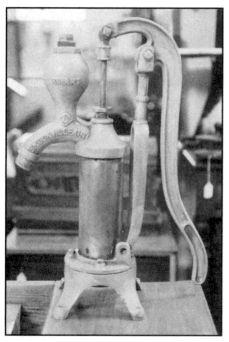

Hand pump, the kind that would have been found in Dennice's farm home.

The summer storms. There was always a calm before a storm. You could see the dark clouds building. I know the farmers would watch those clouds, fearing hail. They could tell by the look of the clouds if hail was coming. I remember one hailstorm. It had been a very hot day, and when the storm hit, the whole crop was wiped out. It took about twelve minutes. Then it was really calm again.

In the summertime, my mom would take lunch to my dad who was working in the field. She'd put everything in a cardboard box to take to him. Coffee in quart sealers with newspaper around to keep the coffee hot. They didn't have tin foil. They didn't have Saran Wrap. There was waxed paper to wrap the sandwiches.

I never had a baby-sitter. I can remember the first time we were left at home alone. I would have been ten or eleven. My parents went out and turned off the power at the power pole. Power hadn't been there that long and I think there was a fear that maybe we were safer with the power off.

We were on a party line. The telephone really did connect us to the community. During seeding or harvest it was not unusual for a farmer to get on the line and interrupt whoever was talking, and tell them to get off the line because he had important business. He might have to order a part because he had a breakdown. People thought nothing of this. Farm business was important business. Some people talked on the phone a lot more than others. And everybody listened in on everybody else but nobody admitted they did.

I remember the cream separator and I remember washing the damn thing. I remember washing all those small parts and pouring hot water over all that metal. We had a cistern with a pump to the kitchen, a hand pump. Mom used to heat wash water in big galvanized tubs on the cook stove. A gas-operated motor ran the washing machine. There was always the fear of getting your hand or arm caught in the wringer. I can remember the Javex being in dark-orange glass bottles. Our Javex was kept in a cupboard at the bottom of the stairs in the basement and it was my job to carry that bottle of Javex upstairs on wash-

Mrs. Stewart's Liquid Bluing, used in the fifties to get whites whiter.

day. I was told to be really careful, because if I ever dropped that bottle and it broke, the Javex could eat through just about anything.

▷ **Giuliana (Julia), born in 1944 in Italy**
  came to Canada in 1953 and grew up in Michel, British Columbia

In Italy, my dad used to make bricks. He did that for twenty-eight years. My mom's sister was in Canada and she would write and say, "Come out here. It's good. You've got a big family. It's not as bad as it is over there with all of the kids." My dad thought it over a lot and eventually everybody said, "Sure, let's go for it."

My dad came over in 1951 to work in the coal mines. We came two years later—my mom and six kids. There were four girls and two boys. I'm the fourth in the family. I was nine years old when we came. I still have my little stub from the ticket on the boat. We landed in Halifax. And we got to BC on July 1, 1953.

None of us spoke English when we got here. My dad didn't

either. Because all the Italians lived in this little town he didn't have to learn. Just "yes," "please," "thank you," "hello" and "good-bye." That was it.

In Italy when you had a couple of extra eggs, you went to the store, gave them the eggs and they would give you some tomato paste or maybe a bundle of spaghetti. That's how it was in Natal, where we shopped. If you brought six eggs, you'd get a slab of butter or whatever. It was the Italian way because they were all Italian. It was like Little Italy.

We had chickens and pigs, we made our own wine, salami, everything. We had potatoes from the back and the front of the house.

When I wasn't in school, I was helping my mom—laundry, cleaning windows, stuff like that. We had big galvanized tubs and a washboard and we had bars of soap, and we'd wash our clothes in there. We would have a special tub for my dad's clothes. They were black from the mines. I remember when they came home, all you would see was their eyes. They'd be just black. Can you imagine breathing in that coal dust like they did? Year in and year out. He was fifty-two when he came here and worked in the mines until he was sixty-four.

For drying the clothes, if it wasn't too windy, we'd hang them on the line outside. If it was windy, the dust from the coal mine would hit the clothes and they'd be black by the time you brought them in. We used to have a garage and a long porch where we had lines and could hang clothes on windy days. We had the kind of iron that you lift up the top and put the coals inside. And that's how we ironed. We never had an ironing board. Just used the table. Which is how I still do it.

And I'd do dishes. We had a well in the back and we'd pump up the water and bring it in and heat it on the stove. We had a pot-bellied stove to keep the house warm.

I can remember Dad would buy us shoes one size too big so we would grow into them the next year. There was no money around.

▷ **Anita, born in 1946**
grew up in Vancouver, British Columbia

The fifties were a happy time. Vancouver had a much smaller population. It was with horror and disgust that news accounts of the crimes in New York and Chicago, for example, were received by my parents and their friends, our neighbours.

Our lives were simple: my father rode the bus daily to his job—few people could afford cars in those days—and my mother was an active participant on the PTA (Parent-Teacher Association). With no brothers or sisters, I believed then, and still do, that I was very lucky. Not only did I enjoy much sharing with my parents, but was frequently included in their social life. Card and board games, Ping-Pong, picnics at Stanley Park: all done on a shoestring budget. I recall asking my mum once why she and Dad never went out. Her reply: "Because we don't have money for bus fare."

We didn't have to lock the front door if we were out back and windows were frequently left open on really warm days. Kids could leave their bikes unattended in their yards, at the ball diamond and outside the corner store, and they would always be there when the owner came back. It was great.

▷ **Ed, born in 1946**
grew up in Saskatoon, Saskatchewan

I had a different life. On average, I spent nine months in the city and three months on the farm each year. So I had the best or worst of both worlds, depending on your perspective. My father operated a farm with his brother and he also had a rural mail business. He delivered bread and gasoline and hauled grain and all those kind of things. The original farm is part of the land we recently bought, along with some other farms, thirty miles from downtown Saskatoon.

So I lived in the city and went to school there except for grade one, when, because of the polio epidemic, we stayed out on the farm in an attempt to not get it but that didn't work, I got it anyway. I had paralysis of the throat and couldn't eat or swallow. If I drank things, they'd come out my nose. I was hospitalized for quite some time in 1953. Then it just went away, as it does. Recently, I was getting checked by a doctor in a medical and he was tapping on my knee and he said, "You had polio, didn't you?" He could tell by my responses.

My mother had very bad polio when she was younger and one of her legs was shorter than the other. Both my older sister and my mother had TB. (I have two sisters, one two years younger and one six years older.) I gather my sister must have had TB fairly young because I can't remember her being sick. She spent some time in the sanitarium in Saskatoon though.

I probably had much more to do with doctors than many kids because I had three eye operations, tonsillitis, polio, and I had pneumonia three times, so more than most kids I ended up interfacing with the medical profession. I had a squint, so I had eye surgery and because in those days they believed in eye exercises, I remember going to the doctor everyday for two or three years and doing eye exercises with this machine.

I had encephalitis and my parents weren't able to see me. This was in the old City Hospital. They'd come to the outside and talk to me at an open window. I was afraid of needles so I'd get up in the morning and walk the hospital for the whole day, because if I came back to my room they'd give me the needles. Eventually they'd catch me.

My dad was out farming with his brother, he was the dealer for North Star Gas, he was hauling grain and he had the Royal Mail route so I spent some time with him but because he was always busy I spent more time with my mother. Ours was a very traditional family and my mom never worked outside the home. I never remember them fighting, ever.

We went out about twice a year to a Chinese restaurant or else we'd go to the King George Hotel and my mother would have breaded veal cutlets on their anniversary. Sometimes on Fridays we'd get fish and chips.

During the Hungarian Revolution, my family took in two Hungarians, Steve and Zoli. Zoli taught me how to tie a tie better than any man I've seen. To this day I can tie a tie better than anybody. They were engineering students. There'd been three of them but only two of them got across the bridge coming out of Hungary. The other one was killed. I remember very clearly the first night at supper time, my mother starting to teach them English. She would teach them something and after that if they couldn't come up with the name for something they wanted, she wouldn't pass it to them. If they wanted ketchup, well, they had to learn "ketchup" or they wouldn't get it. They learned very quickly.

Out on the farm at the start there were coal oil lamps and later a pump run by a one-cylinder external combustion Briggs and Stratton engine. Then we got a wind charger, a thirty-two-volt system with a wind charger and battery. It wasn't until after I left that they got electricity.

My dad had the first truck out there, for his business. I can't remember not having a car, and the first one was a '51 Pontiac that I subsequently bought from my dad. I think he got that relatively new. We had horses, of course, because he had the mail route; in the wintertime the only way to do it was with horses.

There was no phone on the farm, although after a while we got a rural line that wasn't attached to the provincial grid. It was a collection of neighbours cobbled together with the lines running on the barbed-wire fence and regular phone wire. One neighbour at the very end had a Sask Tel line so people would phone them and they would phone you.

When I was a kid there was no running water. We had an outhouse which, in fact, we just burnt down this year. The only thing I ever really built was the farm outhouse. When we bought all that property, we burnt down all the old buildings and buried them.

If we went out to the farm in the winter, which was not very often, we used the outhouse. Of course, there was no choice. I do remember that in the summertime we did have something in the house for when you had to tinkle during the night. As a kid you wouldn't need that very much. More for older guys.

▷ **Sandy, born in 1946**
grew up in Winnipeg, Manitoba

I grew up in the Fort Rouge area of Winnipeg, and was born a year to the day after the United Nations were formed. I had an older brother, five years older. My mom and dad worked at real estate and insurance. She really did a lot of work and didn't get a lot of credit for it. She kept all the files, paid the bills, kept it all in order.

Our street was a Protestant-type of street; very keep to yourself, mind your own business, keep the door shut, don't loiter on the front porch. A couple of streets over were the wartime houses and the two didn't mix at all. The wartime houses were a completely different world. The people were mostly from another country. I had some friends there who were from England and several others who were English war brides. Some were disappointed. There was this other neighbourhood on the other side that was wealthy and Jewish. And I was kind of sandwiched between. I tended to hang out with the people who hung out on their porches in the wartime houses.

▷ **Candace, born in 1946**
grew up in Edmonton, Alberta

For a few years my dad worked on the railroad, an engineer. Then he started his own maintenance business in Edmonton. My mom was a nurse and for quite a few years she worked in a hospital in Edmonton. I have a sister three years younger.

My grandmother lived with us for my whole life at home. She was

Candace with her grandmother, her mother and her sister in 1950.

wonderful. She baked bread and buns. Everything was home-baked. She was a fabulous cook. I remember her fresh cinnamon buns. You'd come home from school and smell them baking. And I could just kick myself for not learning to bake from her. I was really close to my grandmother because my mother worked. She was always there for us. So we weren't latchkey kids. My granny made a lot of my clothes. She was a seamstress and I have a picture of myself and my sister in little party dresses with the little pinafore aprons. We always had little gloves when we went to church, and hats, white socks and black shoes with straps.

We used to go to Woodward's Food Floor every Saturday to buy groceries with my mom. And the groceries would be delivered, we didn't bring them home with us. You'd pay for it and go home and they'd be delivered.

I remember the street photographers. That must have been quite a business. They'd take your picture and you'd get a coupon to claim it when it was developed.

We had a coal chute in the house. And I can also remember in North Vancouver at my aunt's place the ice guy used to come because they just had an icebox and he had these big clamps to put the ice in the icebox.

We had a wringer washing machine. My dad would always say, "Now be careful of that wringer." So one time I went down, it was in the basement, and I washed something and, of course, I had to put it through the wringer. And sure enough, my arm went right through the wringer too. My dad could hear me screaming and he immediately turned off the power.

Almost every Christmas, I got something—something communicable. I had measles, I had chicken pox and one year I had a flu of some kind. I was in bed for about two weeks and I remember my mom massaging my arms and legs. I don't know what it was. Invariably though, I'd have something at Christmastime and be so upset.

▷ **Ken, born in 1947 in Victoria**
grew up just outside Edmonton, Alberta

No question, Dad was the boss. He was out of town quite a bit because he was a welder on the pipeline. Mother was in charge when he was away but she deferred to him when he was home. Although my mother worked for a good portion of her life, she was working not so much to survive but more for a little better quality of life.

We had relatives scattered all over. There was maybe twenty, twenty-five family gatherings throughout the year. I had four sisters, two older and two younger and I had about fifty-two girl cousins, too. Growing up with that many sisters, and always having four or five boarders who were all taking nursing, with that many women around, I ended up learning a lot of sewing, ironing. Strangely enough I seemed to be the only one who enjoyed it so I did a lot of the cooking and a lot of the housework. Other than that, my chores were basically take out the garbage, shovel the walk, weed the garden. Sometimes I'd trade with one or the other of my sisters for their week of doing the dishes and cooking for my week to take out the garbage. Being disciplined meant being given a lot of extra chores. Gave you time to think about your indiscretions.

▷ **Louise, born in 1947**
grew up in Slocan, British Columbia

My dad was a partner in a sawmill and my mom did the books for the sawmill at home. They later sold the sawmill and my dad went into partnership in another sawmill and then worked for the village for awhile. Mom sometimes did laundry for the construction crews that were building the highway. Dad was head of the household. He was from Denmark and the macho-male type. Mom didn't have much of a voice although she took care of discipline. Dad wouldn't know about it unless he happened to show up at the time.

We had electricity and running water but I can remember my aunt, my mom's sister, who lived out of town about three miles, having gas lamps. Their first power was from a generator plant out at the creek. We didn't have a telephone until the late fifties. There was a telephone in town that went through the post office, an old-fashioned one where the operator would listen in when you were talking.

I remember the train station. On the left-hand side, just inside the door, was a long counter and the station agent was behind the counter. The waiting room had a high wood stove, you put the wood in at the top. And the room had real wood panelling. I remember there was a boat on the lake that pulled the trains on a barge across to Silverton and New Denver. That stopped not so very long ago.

There was a meat market in town run by Japanese people who had come from the internment camps. And there was a big grocery store that also had clothes. There used to be big barrels of peanuts, like wooden oak barrels. There were other containers where you got flour and other stuff, bulk items. The sidewalks were wood. I can remember coming out of the store and losing money down the slots in the sidewalk.

My mom made mustard and onion plasters when we were sick. She put the onion mix between two cloths and heated it up, then put it on. I think they worked, or at least you pretended they did, so you wouldn't have to go through that again. I remember sulphur and molasses mixed up as a spring tonic. It kind of cleaned you out after the winter, in both directions. That was one thing her mother did for her so she figured we all needed it too, I guess. Tasted terrible. And halibut liver oil pills that you used to burp back. And cod liver oil, of course.

▷ **Greg, born in 1947**
grew up on the Tsartlip Reserve on Vancouver Island, British Columbia

I was born here on the Tsartlip Reserve. I have two sisters and six brothers. I'm second oldest. My father worked in the coal yard in Victoria. He drove a truck and packed coal. That's the first thing I remember, him coming home from working in the coal yard. My mother was a housewife and at that time was knitting Indian sweaters. She did that all the time and she sold them on a regular basis. That supplemented what my father was making because he didn't get much pay working in the coal yards. I can remember going into Victoria to sell sweaters and sometimes the buyers would come out here. We had to card the wool, we had to tease it and then we had to stand there and hold it while she unravelled it and made it into a ball. I remember doing it for years and years. She got the wool from local farmers. She had to wash the wool. About three days' work. It was a lot of work. She was quite old when she quit knitting. She had arthritis. Sometimes she'd go and pick potatoes. She worked hard.

We got electricity when I was seven or eight. That'd be 1954, 1955. Before that we had coal oil lamps. We had outdoor toilets and a well for water.

At home it was mostly my dad who disciplined us. I can remember him scolding us. He would explain why he was doing it and he would also explain a lot of our teachings. He talked about schooling, conduct and appearance and he taught us respect. In the community it was understood that if you got out of hand, our aunts and uncles could speak to us about it. So there was a fair amount of that. We weren't really allowed to get involved in the Indian ceremonies. Except from time to time we'd be taught a little about it.

My parents always had visitors. We would sit and listen, we weren't supposed to move, while they would have tea. It was a humbling experience. If we did move, one of them would say something to us. It wouldn't be the parents, it would be the elderly ladies. Because of that we didn't like them to come and visit. When you stop and think about it, there was a lot of teachings that were given to us by our parents, by our uncles and aunts and grandparents, and some of our grandaunts and granduncles. So it was always reinforced. It wasn't just in the home. It was outside too. If we were outside playing, they would remind us— talk to us, ask us what we were doing.

I remember when I was two years old, I used to wander the reserve. I'd wander quite a distance, it must have been a quarter of a mile, and go visit my grandmother. She was the one who delivered me into this world.

▷ **Thelma, born in 1948**
  grew up in Vancouver, British Columbia

When I was very young, say five or so, we had no phone. Once I was badly cut on the head and Mother lay me on the bathroom floor while she ran to the only neighbour who had a phone. The doctor and his father, also a doctor, came to the house and stitched me up. Later we did get a phone. It was a two-party line but only rang on one party at a time, not like the prairie rural lines that had code rings.

We had no car at the time—not until I was eleven or twelve, but my aunt and her husband were very generous about coming from North Vancouver and taking us out for Sunday drives to White Rock, Boundary Bay and even Penticton once.

▷ **Karen, born in 1949**
grew up in Victoria, British Columbia

My mother died when I was three, and about two or three months prior to her going into the hospital, I went to live with relatives at Duncan. My brother was eight and going to school and my father couldn't be a single parent for both of us, with me not yet in school. There was lots of emotional turmoil. I only saw my father and brother on weekends. We were poor and didn't have a car so he came up on the bus to get me on weekends. That took a long time in those days.

My deafness was diagnosed when I was four or four and a half. My brother was born deaf. It was probably a recessive gene in my family. Both my parents probably carried the gene but didn't know it at the time.

I came back home to live when I was five to go to kindergarten. Kindergarten wasn't mandatory then but there were lots of private ones. I got kicked out of five kindergartens. I was a bit of a devil, for lots of reasons. I think I had a real sense of what I wanted to do and it didn't necessarily follow the rules. I think my deafness played a major role although I couldn't analyze it at that time. I got my first hearing aid just before going into kindergarten so that was a major deal. And in those days they were very visible. I had two little boxes with cords— probably took over most of my body! There wasn't much in the way of in-service at the time, except for what my father would advocate for. He was a tremendous advocate. But he didn't have any exposure to textbooks or anything so he was going by his own parental intuition.

I was very independent. I would get up in the morning and get breakfast going, make my own lunch and get off to school. We were expected to take part in making dinner. Potatoes had to be peeled and in the water ready to be boiled by the time my father walked off the bus. Doing household chores was a strong expectation. And it wasn't done necessarily for an allowance. It's what you did to be an integral part of the family.

▷ **Anne, born in 1949 in Winnipeg**
grew up in Calgary, Winnipeg, Vancouver, Victoria and Edmonton

I have two older brothers and two younger brothers. I'm in the middle, the only girl. Mom was a homemaker for most of the time. After the oldest three children left home and she just had the younger two at home in university, she went to work for two or three years. She worked in the Registrar's office of the University of Manitoba. All the time we were growing up, she didn't work outside the home at all, although she did prior to her marriage. She worked for an insurance company in Winnipeg. She had two university degrees, a Bachelor of Arts and a Bachelor of Education.

Anne and her four brothers at their Calgary home in the spring of 1953.

My father was a chartered accountant and he worked for the Hudson's Bay retail stores. I was born in Winnipeg and we moved to Calgary for a short time, then back to Winnipeg and then back to Calgary when I was five. We lived in West Vancouver for three years from the time I was six until I was nine, and then in Victoria for three years, and then we moved to Edmonton for five years until I was about sixteen and then we moved to Calgary for the last two years of my high school. I stayed there to go to university and that's where I met and married my husband.

We were transferred—that's the word they used. It was a promotion each time but that company, along with other department stores and corporations, moved people regularly. My mother didn't talk about it then and she doesn't talk about it now. But what she thought about it—what I would guess—is that she didn't like it very much. The moves were very frequent and all the work was left to her. My father would hear the word that he had been transferred and shortly after that he would fly off to the new location and we'd all be left there for several months. He'd come home on weekends but there would be a period at first when Mother would be single parent when he had already moved to the new location and she would have to organize the whole move. Of course, because it was a company move, a company moving van was supplied and so on. She didn't have to physically do the packing but she had to supervise it all and arrange for all of the utilities to be unhooked and hooked up in the new location. We would move en masse to the new location and there would be another period of disruptions. We might be in a rental home for a short time before we found a home which we would purchase and there would be a period of disruption that would maybe involve two moves, one into the rental accommodation and then one into the more permanent—and I use the word permanent loosely—location for the next couple of years. She would have to supervise all the unpacking, getting connected to the new community, all the schools for us. It was a lot of work for her to move.

Of course, Mother was the one who was at home so I think it was lonely for her. She worked really hard with the five of us in the home and I think it was harder for her just because she didn't have the time to make acquaintances, make friends, get some new company. Whereas, of course, my father would just be plugged into the new organization, his new store and his new location and he would have colleagues at work. My impression is that they always had lots of friends and did a lot of socializing as a couple. I don't recall her having friends of her own because she simply didn't have time to do that.

When I was small, moving was very much a part of our life. Even a year to a very young child is forever and they can just drop their friends and their environment and pick up again somewhere else. As long as I had my family with me, which I always did, I was secure and happy. When I got older

Anne sits on the step of one of her own homes amid packing boxes.

though, my attachments to my friends were much closer and I was very unhappy to move. I particularly remember, in my last years of high school, I stayed in Calgary but my parents made another move to Winnipeg and took my two youngest brothers with them because they were still living at home. They were junior high age and they were very unhappy to move because they had been in Edmonton for five years and Calgary for, I would guess, about the same period of time, so they hadn't experienced as many moves. They were really attached to their social structure in Calgary.

There was never any question of the transfer being accepted and my father was always very excited and happy about it. Not just that it was a promotion but that it was a new adventure, a chance to set off again. He always viewed these very positively. I don't think my mother did, but that was never voiced.

We were all well-behaved children and were expected to behave, do certain things, not do other things. It was common at that time that if we'd done something bad, like going out after school when we had been told not to, blatant disobedience, then we were told, "Wait until your father gets home." He would come home and he would be the one who would mete out the punishment. The punishment was being spanked. At that time, I didn't think anything of it. I certainly didn't like it, none of us did. It was emotionally very upsetting when one got a spanking but none of us was really physically hurt and my understanding was every family did this. You always assume what happens in your family is what happens in other families. I think I would've talked to friends about it and the same thing would have happened to them. Now, even if you're not hurting them, I would never turn my child over my knee and spank their bottom! I would never lay a hand on my children.

Mom would spank on occasion, but for the most part spanking was reserved for when we were really bad and my father would do it. He was the ultimate disciplinarian with the final word. I remember once when I was about ten and it was my birthday. Mom always planned an elaborate birthday party for us every year. For my birthday party, I wanted to have a sleep-over. My mother and I had planned for this and then she told my dad after it had all been planned and guests invited. She told me that I couldn't have the party because my father didn't like sleep-overs for a reason that was never explained. But his was the ultimate word and because he said there would not be one, there wasn't one. There was no question, no discussion. I was bitterly, bitterly disappointed and I ran away for a couple of hours. Looking back on it now, I think that it was my father's fear of anything physical or sexual at all. He would think, What would all those little kids be doing together at a sleep-over? I'm sure that's what it was. And I may have had some kind of feeling about that at the time. But I was so disappointed.

When people visited there were adult activities and conversation and then there was children's activities and conversation and very rarely would those things be together.

My brothers did the outdoor chores. I've never cut a lawn. Never. Outside work was males' work and I never helped with that. However, inside the house, I learned to cook from my mother and I'm very grateful to her for that. She didn't teach any of my brothers to cook.

▷ **Linda C., born in 1949**
grew up in Calgary and Sylvan Lake, Alberta

I have three younger sisters. We were a traditional family, I would say. Dad went to work, but Mom also went to work. My dad, in the very early days, was a carpenter and then in later years he became a postman. My mother worked in restaurants and later for a care home, a hospital for the mentally challenged, or handicapped as they were called then. The more traditional family was that mom stayed home and looked after the kids. But my mother was a very independent thinker. She was in the army, one of the very few women who joined the army back then. And of course, because we were a poor family on the prairies, Mom had to work.

Linda on her tricycle in Calgary, circa 1954.

When I was in grade one and two we lived in Calgary. Bowness was on the western perimeter. Back then it was real prairie. Our neighbourhood was a whole new subdivision. I can remember vacant lots. There were huge hills out behind our place where we used to wander and pick wild flowers. Years later I went back and it was totally developed.

Then we went to Sylvan Lake, a small town ten miles outside Red Deer. My parents bought a motel there. Our living conditions went from being reasonably civilized to being—well I guess— small-town Alberta. We didn't have inside toilets. We had a milkman who came and delivered the milk with a horse and buggy. Remember when the milkman would bring the milk and the cream had all risen to the top? And we had an iceman too, who delivered ice for the icebox. We had a telephone where you'd ring and— we were number 139—Myrtle at the Central Exchange would connect you to whomever you wanted to talk to. For me it was a throwback. In the city we'd had all the amenities—running water and all that good stuff. I remember at the lake, we didn't have sewers so there was a bucket under the kitchen sink where all the water drained to and then you'd have to carry it out. A slop pail—that's what it was called.

We had a wringer washer. I remember getting my hand caught in the wringer once and thinking I'd broken all my fingers. My parents operated a motel so I used to have to help, even as an eight year old, stripping sheets off of beds and doing the laundry. Summer and winter my mom hung the sheets on the line and, of course, at thirty or forty below, they'd freeze. I don't know how they ever dried because they'd be frozen when you'd bring them in. She'd hang them inside for a while just to finish them off. I don't know when they invented the modern-day washer but we didn't have one when I left home, and when I went to university I didn't have a clue how to operate one. I knew how to operate a wringer washer but not one of those.

One thing we did have was a floor polisher with the two rotating heads. But my mother also sewed us little square cloth things that we could put on our feet. After she waxed the floor, rather than getting out the floor polisher, she would have us slide up and down and shine the floor. We thought that was just the greatest fun. My sister and I, we'd slide back and forth with these little slippers on our feet.

The big scare, of course, when we were young—well, I can re-member laying awake at night thinking about how my parents had to build a bomb shelter in case the Russians came. And how much food we'd need and what it would be like, in my imagination, living in a bomb shelter. That was a very real concern as a child. We were very scared of the Russians.

I remember what was probably the forerunner of credit cards. It was called revolving credit. We went to visit the clothing store where my granny worked, The Parisienne in Calgary, twice a year. Once in the spring at Easter and then again just before we went back to school in September. In the spring we got a new Easter dress, a new Easter hat and new white shoes. In the fall it was back-to-school clothing. As my parents were poor—and wasn't everyone back then?—they could not afford to pay for the stuff we bought all at once. The way revolving credit worked was you made monthly installment payments for the next number of months, usually six, I believe, to pay off the amount you owed.

Every fall my mother bought a box of peaches, a box of pears, a box of plums and canned them and we picked berries and she made

Linda, her sister and her mother on a Calgary street in front of The Parisienne. Photo taken by a street photographer.

jam and she put up pickles. She'd spend weeks and weeks in September just canning. My home was so regular. I don't know if maybe this is a prairie thing. I can tell you on any given day of the week what we were going to be eating. Saturday night was hamburgers and chocolate milk and "Hockey Night in Canada," Sunday was roast beef, Monday my mother made chicken noodle soup while she washed, and Tuesday she ironed and Friday she cleaned house and we had fish 'n' chips. It was a weekly routine. I could tell you what a standard prairie meal was: pork chops, creamed corn, mashed potatoes and applesauce. And the vegetables were boiled to death and the pork chops were cooked until they were like shoe leather. I do remember corn and peas and carrots. Mom had cauliflower as a treat now and then but us kids wouldn't eat it. I never even knew what a zucchini was until I was in university. And always potatoes, that was probably because my father was a potato man. Rice was unheard of. I remember my parents going to a New Year's party and the people must have served Chinese food. My father would not eat Chinese food. I remember them coming home and him complaining bitterly and my mother having to cook him a meal at two in the morning because he hadn't eaten anything all night.

When we moved to Sylvan Lake we had an outdoor toilet. My mother was not too pleased with that. It was pretty cold going out to it in winter. First, we had a little pot in the house and then my mother had my father build a closet and we put a chemical toilet in it. Basically a big bucket with a seat on it. You'd put chemicals in it and carry it out on a regular basis. Saturday night was bath night. Started with the littlest one in a tin tub out in the laundry room. We didn't have hot water so Mom boiled water to put in the tub. Then she and Dad bathed last—Mom and then Dad. Every Saturday night.

I think I learned the facts of life from my cousin. At least I got some explanation from her. One Sunday afternoon, my parents sat me and my younger sister down and tried to teach us the facts of life. They had a record that was put out by some monks teaching family values. They played this record and the monks went through this in a very nice way, and at the end of that, my mother said, "So, how much of that did you know?" Of course my sister said she didn't know any of it, this was all new to her. And of course I said, "Oh, I knew it all." Then of course my mother went into a tailspin. "It's Vicki, it's your cousin Vicki, isn't it?" The record wasn't very explicit—more how important it was to get married and have Catholic kids and all that stuff.

I can remember my parents talking about a couple who were "living together." They were shacking up. And that was just awful. You did not do that sort of thing.

▷ Dennis, born in 1949
grew up in Burnaby, British Columbia

My brothers and sister can say that I was an only child because they were all born in the thirties and I came along in 1949. When I was born, they were seventeen, eighteen years old. By the time I was six years old, they were off, married, starting to have families of their own. In fact my oldest niece is only seven years younger than me. So I was really a postwar baby boomer. I was a preemie. Weighed four pounds, ten ounces, and spent a few weeks in an incubator. My uncle tells me I was no bigger than his hand. He could hold me in his hand quite nicely. Not quite the case today.

I remember visiting my grandmother on the farm in Saskatchewan when I was five years old and being bitten by a chicken in the henhouse. I remember travelling across the country. My second oldest brother was the driver. So there was my brother, my mom, my dad and myself and we were driving from Vancouver to Saskatchewan, but in those days you went through the States 'cause the roads were much better.

I think my one memory from the earlier years would have been the winter of 1954-55 in Vancouver. It was an exceptionally cold year. As a little kid I remember the snow was so high. It looked like it was about three feet deep on the front lawn. That's the kind of thing that was never repeated again in the greater Vancouver area. So it was a highly unusual winter.

As far as I can remember, my mother never had a job outside the home. When I came home from school, she was there. She was the disciplinarian. My dad didn't take an interest in that.

I grew up in a new neighbourhood, constructed around 1949, in north Burnaby. The houses were maybe 1,200 square feet and were supposed to be affordable housing. During the postwar boom, it was a massive housing development. I think at that time you would have that kind of development going on all over the place. Families would look at that kind of neighbourhood as upper scale. A lot of people went on to prestigious positions with large corporations. As they left, other people came in and the nature of the neighbourhood changed and became essentially a middle-class neighbourhood.

My family wasn't rich. My dad never owned a car and was never able to travel. He worked for what is now the Greater Vancouver Regional District; then it was called the Greater Vancouver Water Board. His regular job was as a diver's tender. He was in charge of the hard hat divers who went underwater. He had to make sure there was communication going on, that the air was going down to them and that they were generally okay. The diver would be under the water for two or three hours. He and the crew that he worked with were responsible for most of the major water supply systems that were installed in the Lower Mainland from the 1950s onward. Practically anybody who drinks water in Vancouver is getting it through a pipe that was installed at three o'clock in the morning by my dad and that work crew. He was also involved in the construction of the Seymour River Dam. When that kind of work wasn't around, it was other jobs, a "getting by" type of deal. We were never rich by any stretch of the imagination. But they used to say, everybody who had a car went to work with peanut butter sandwiches, at least we had roast beef sandwiches.

▷ **Dan, born in 1949**
grew up on a ranch near Lundbreck in southern Alberta

I was born in Edmonton but we lived in the town of Devon, Alberta. We moved to the Pincher Creek area, to a ranch near Lundbreck, a town of about a hundred people, shortly after I was born. My grandfather had been a rancher in that area.

I was the only child until my brother was born about seven years later. Dad happened to be working in the oilpatch at the time for a supply company. Mom always kept a big garden, still does. Bigger than she really needs now.

As far as I can remember my dad always had a car. He had a Model A in the fifties. He had lots of fun driving that. I remember going down the road in it and one of the wheels coming off and rolling down the road ahead of us.

▷ **George, born in 1950**
   grew up in Vanderhoof and Prince George, British Columbia

I was born a week before Christmas in 1950. My mom was delighted when she carried me home, a week later, that they had installed lights on the old bridge over the Nechako River for the pedestrian walkway that ran along one side of it. It was a cold winter and it was about twenty below zero, as she carried me nearly two miles home, to our rented cabin on the south side of town in an auto-court. That's what they called motels in those days.

A few years later my dad arranged for us to spend some time with him out at Kenny Dam, which was under construction and where he worked as a carpenter. We lived in a tent there and I remember Euclids and Cats looked like toys and the men, no larger than ants. I was thrilled when we took a walk and those big Euclids drove by. I never forgot the sound of their engines. I heard them again in 1975, when I started working with skidders, and realized that those same Detroit diesels were powering them, too.

In 1954, we moved from the dusty little town of Vanderhoof to the dusty little bigger town of Prince George. There was very little pavement on the streets in those days and some of the sidewalks were made of wood. Dad got a job as a powerhouse operator out at the US radar base, Baldy Hughes, thirty miles south of town. We settled into a small house in the Island Cache area of town by the river. Mom and us kids (I had a younger brother and an older sister and brother) had come to town on the train and Dad had driven his car down. The car was a 1938 Chev. That night it was quite cold and the next morning the frost plugs from the engine were lying on the ground. We loved that old car, but it never ran for us again. Later, Dad bought an Austin Brave, and he and the other guys took turns driving and riding on their daily commute to work. He eventually got a little trailer and moved it out to the base, so he could put in his forty-eight hours in three days and then be home for three days. They worked eight hours on and eight hours off and the trailer gave him a decent place to sleep. When he got extra

Saturday shifts, he would sometimes take me along for the day, starting when I was about six years old. I just loved that! I learned how everything worked, learned how to take the hourly log and the half-hourly checks. I learned how to start an engine and how to throw the load onto it at just the right time by watching the cycles meter and shut down the other engine. I carried a wiping rag in my belt, just like my dad did, to wipe away any oil I found leaking anywhere and learned how to spot any trouble before it could develop into something serious. I can still hear the pounding of those three big Vivian Marine diesels. Later, when they upgraded the radar, they replaced them with five new National diesels that could put out a million watts of power.

Back at home, my older brother was in charge of the firewood and splitting the kindling, while it was my job to break up the big chunk coal into smaller pieces that would fit into the heater and bring in a full scuttle every night during the cold weather. I also had to clean out the clinkers and take out the ashes. I guess our house was a bit cold, because we had a kitchen wood stove and a wood heater as well as a coal heater in the living room. We would keep the house banked up with snow all winter and always had big icicles hanging from the eaves. Since I was the smallest child, it was me who had to crawl down the well and tie newspapers around the water pipe with string to keep it from freezing up. Thinking back now that well cribbing must have only been about eighteen-inches square. It was a fairly tight fit even for me, back then.

It must have been about 1955 when Mom started working part-time for Wilson, King and Fretwell, a law firm, as a stenographer. I think she just worked when Dad was home on days off and a half-day on Saturdays. Sometimes on Saturdays she would take me along with her too. All she had to do was give me some paper and pencils while she worked away at her typewriter with the dictaphone headset on. It was she who bought a washing machine, then a fridge and a propane stove. Any Saturday that she didn't work at the office the house would be filled with the aroma of baking bread, pies, cookies and cakes. In the summer she loved to put the bread out on the back porch in the sun to rise. I really loved my mother and whatever she was doing, I had to be there helping her, whether it was knitting, sewing or cooking. I learned a terrific amount from her. She took me to concerts, operettas and shows, because I would sit still and enjoy them. Dad was great with us kids too. He really spent his free time with us, always teaching us about whatever it was that he was doing or just spending time playing with us. Mom always read to us before we went to bed and took us to church. She loved going for walks and the smell of fresh-sawn lumber. That was good because there were several sawmills close by and they used to stack the lumber in tall piles to dry. To get to town, we had to walk a couple of miles and across the huge CNR yards. Dad loved trains and even got us rides on a steam locomotive before they went out of service. Sunday afternoons we often went for drives in the country and had a picnic or we would make the trip back to Vanderhoof to visit Dad's parents. These were always an adventure, because roads then were nothing like what we have today.

Highway 16, as it's called now, was then the Northern Trans-provincial Highway and by today's standards, well, it's hard to compare. Sometimes you could get through and sometimes you couldn't! Some places were great long puddles and other places were just a mass of muddy ruts. If you didn't choose the right one, you might not make it through. It was not uncommon for everyone to get out of the car to help push it through places like that. Cars had to slow down when meeting other vehicles and often pull over to the side a bit to pass and to keep flying rocks to a minimum. Common courtesy was something that was just second nature to people then. If you saw someone in trouble, you stopped to see if you could be of any assistance. Hitchhikers were picked up and could be trusted. Honour was a word that meant something. People had a sense of humour too. It wasn't uncommon to see a little sign posted at big puddles in the road which read "Good Fishing" or "No Fishing" or "Boats for Rent." In the wintertime, part way up any steep hill, you'd find an orange painted box with sand in it and a shovel at the side of the road for people who spun out trying to get up the hill. On long hills there would be two or three of them. After the government paved that road and then they started constructing a brand new highway, the one we have today, there were some trouble spots. On Peden Hill just leaving Prince George to the west, they had to have a Cat there to pull vehicles up the hill one at a time if they couldn't make it on their own because it was so muddy, and at Mud River, the detour was so bad that some vehicles had to be pulled down the hill, too.

I remember that we took in a Hungarian family for a few months one year. They were a grandmother, her son, his wife and two children. They spoke very little English but us kids started picking up Hungarian. It must have been quite crowded in our little house but they stayed until the fellow found a job and got them a house of their own. They were very appreciative to be there.

The rent for our old, small three-bedroom house was $40 per month. In 1959, we rented a much larger three-bedroom house with hardwood floors and a basement and large bright windows in the living room for $70 a month. The following year, Dad had a house built for Mom that fulfilled her lifelong dream. It and the lot cost $10,500—more than twice his yearly earnings!

▷ **Bruce, born in 1950**
grew up in Winnipeg, Edmonton and Regina

I was born and raised in Winnipeg and my dad was with Uniroyal. In those days it was called the Dominion Rubber Company. He transferred to Edmonton in 1959 and was in Edmonton until 1961, and then we moved to Regina. So I lived in all three Prairie provinces.

I have two brothers and a sister. My brother was born in 1952, my sister in 1955 and my kid brother wasn't born until the seventies. My mom called him the second family. We were all baby boomers, charter members I suppose you could say.

Our life was quite traditional, for the fifties at least. My father went to work. He was a salesman for the Dominion Rubber Company. When we were in Winnipeg, he was in their tire division and I remember him going to work every morning. My mom would have the two of us—my brother and I were close in age, not quite two years apart. So she had her hands full with two rambunctious boys. My sister came along when I was five. I remember that vividly. We didn't think we were poor but we certainly weren't well off.

I remember every Monday was laundry day and my mom started off with just an old washtub. One of the first things that she persuaded my father to buy was an electric washer. We didn't have a dryer for years. I don't think we got a dryer until the sixties. Mom hung her wash out winter and summer. The ironing would go on for a couple of days.

Our home life was very much centred on the home and grandparents. My father was very close to his family. So when Mom went shopping on Saturday, sometimes we would go with her, but quite often we'd go with Dad over to Grandma's. And that was kind of the regular Saturday visit. Then on Sundays, quite often we would have one of the aunts or uncles over for Sunday dinner. My father was the youngest of twelve children so there were lots of family connections, and still are.

My mom started to work when we got to Edmonton in 1959. That was very unusual then. She was a secretary. I remember thinking when I would go to my friends, What do you mean your mom is at home? Doesn't everybody's mom work? This was in the sixties and by that time I was used to it. But it was still pretty unusual, until the mid-sixties, for women to work outside the home.

▷ **Audrey R., born in 1953**
grew up on a farm near Pelly, Saskatchewan

I have a sister and brother younger than me. My first memories are of having a lot of cousins around all the time. We lived on the farm and my aunts and uncles lived in town, but they farmed too. So our place was kind of a stopping-off point. They'd come to our house for a lot of meals. My grandparents, my mother's parents, lived on our property next to us when I was really small. My grandmother on my dad's side lived in Victoria. After my mom's dad died, Grandma came and lived with us. We were very young and it never dawned on us that it should be any other way.

We lived in a mainly Ukrainian and Russian community. We were the exception being English. My dad never, ever touched garlic. So it was something we'd never experienced at home. But in school you knew there was garlic in those lunch kits. The odour hit you like a ton of bricks. At the fowl suppers there was mostly Ukrainian and Russian food like cabbage rolls, perogies and borscht. I loved it all.

We never toyed with the idea of staying in that town after graduation. You couldn't get a job in a store or restaurant, bank or anything because we didn't speak Russian or Ukrainian, and of course we didn't want to stay on the farm because we recognized it for the expensive hobby that it is.

There was an Indian reserve about ten miles to the south of us, another one further south and one eight miles east of us. On the three reserves there were approximately one thousand natives. The population of the town was about five hundred. I never went to school with the native kids. There was a Catholic mission school on one of the reserves, but I don't know about the other ones. I don't know where they went to school.

Back then you would get long, handwritten letters from relatives. A long distance phone call was when there was bad news. My aunt in Timmins would send us boxes of clothes that her daughter had grown out of. There was a lot of fancy stuff that we wouldn't get otherwise. I remember each year my mom would buy corduroy and flannelette and make three pairs of lined slacks for my sister and I and that's what we wore to school all winter.

I always liked to help outside to avoid house chores. Once my sister and I were to feed the calves. They were pail fed and you had to take the pail to them and make sure they ate. But my dad warned us not to confuse them and feed one of them more than once or they'd die. I was terrified that I might finish one of them off so I got a lipstick and marked each head as he got his pail of milk. My dad was not impressed. He said he'd been culling this registered herd for twenty-five years and look what I'd done to them. Needless to say, I failed farm. Whenever I tried to help outside, he'd tolerate my efforts, then ask, "So now are you ready to go to the house?"

▷ **Bill, born in 1954**
grew up in Rosthern, Saskatchewan, until 1964

I was the middle of five children. Life for me was fairly carefree, although it was a pretty rough period for my folks. My father had taken over a garage that was on pretty shaky ground. That didn't succeed so he worked very hard at a number of jobs to try to keep the family fed. With five growing kids and really not much happening in Saskatchewan at that time he eventually had to go further afield. He went to Edmonton and worked in the auto trade in a garage before he got news of an opportunity in Yellowknife and we moved in 1964.

In Rosthern, my step-grandmother lived right next door. She was a widow, a very austere woman. It was not like we could romp all over her house. But she tried to teach us kids how to paint, I remember that.

To keep things going, Mom did secretarial work. During the war she had worked for CBC radio doing stenographic stuff and a very small amount of broadcast work. Of course, she didn't get much of an opportunity because women on the air was not generally accepted.

I had a number of aunts and uncles who all lived on farms in the area. We were the town family. Every year there would be a great slaughter of pigs, cows and chickens at one of the farms. It got to be a routine each fall and it involved a lot of work. It was a marvelous thing to watch as in the farmhouse kitchen the women were processing sausages, while in the barn, after the butchering was finished, the men gathered around the stove smoking and sharing a bottle while the women finished up in the house. There was a great sense of family on mother's side. I had lots and lots of cousins around all the time. Of course the family was aghast when we left to go north. But it was the best thing my parents could have done and it was a very brave and bold move at the time. All of us have done well and prospered.

Good old golden rule days

For most of us, entering grade one was our first experience in a class-room, our first experience in sustained activity with our peers and our first experience being responsible to an authority other than a family member. Entering grade one was the first major milestone of our lives.

We remember saluting the flag and singing "O Canada" or "God Save the Queen" each morning in the classroom. We remember the straight rows of desks and the equally straight rows of students who lined up for everything. That was us. We remember our teachers, most of them women, and many not long out of school themselves. Until the 1960s, a teaching certificate, earned after one year of teacher training at Normal School, qualified a person to take on the task of imparting knowledge to large classrooms of students—classrooms often filled beyond capacity by the babies born during and after the Second World War. We remember many of those teachers with affection and awe. They made learning magical and inspired us to want to learn more. Others we remember as the tyrants they were.

We learned to read and write in classrooms where silence prevailed during school hours. In our experience, classroom discipline was as real and serious as the Cold War. We learned socialization skills on the playground, some learning to be leaders while others learned how best to follow, while we all suffered the bullies among us.

We experienced many changes in the school systems as governments adapted to increased populations, improvements in roads and advances in transportation. Although I lived in the same place for all of my growing-up years, I attended a country school for two years, then rode a bus daily to a village school for eight years, and spent my last two years of high school being bused to a new centralized high school that served three villages and their outlying communities.

When the Soviet Union sent its first space satellite aloft in 1957, educators on this continent began to agitate for more support from governments and governments listened, easily convinced that the threat of a technologically superior Cold War enemy could be met with an equally educated and technologically adept populace. What this meant for children in the school systems at the time was more change—changes in curriculum and changes in the subjects we were studying.

▷ **Peter P., born in 1935**
  grew up on a farm near Winlaw in southern British Columbia

There were two classrooms. One for grades one to four and another for grades five to nine. There must have been about forty kids in the school. A lot of teachers went through our school because it was a tough place—it was half Russian and half English—and they were always feuding.

There was about a dozen, twelve or fourteen, boys around my age. Probably about the same number of girls. At that time we didn't have a high school close by. We only had up to grade nine. So when I quit school, I figured I had enough schooling. I knew I couldn't go any further so I figured I might as well help my mother at home. In about 1960 they did build a high school in Slocan and then had a school bus taking students back and forth. But this was years after I quit.

▷ **Jim, born in 1937**
grew up in Pipestone, Manitoba

In high school, there'd be grades nine to eleven in one room. Maybe thirty kids with one teacher for all subjects. Discipline was up to the individual teacher and was often corporal punishment, the strap. Sometimes I had it coming, other times I didn't. Once I got it for playing hooky and another time for talking in class. We weren't exactly the best kids in the world but neither were we the worst. We didn't do really bad things. Parents agreed with the punishment most of the time. You knew very well when you did some of these things what the consequences could be, but if you really wanted to do them, it didn't matter!

Looking back now, I remember one of the teachers in particular, and how miserable we made his life. He was only a couple years older than we were in grade eleven. I feel bad about it now but at the time it was kind of fun, you know. It was a lot of years before he'd speak to me again. A few years after I met him on the street and he wasn't very— well, he hadn't forgiven me yet. But he had, the last time I talked to him. Mind you, that was a lot of years later!

While I was going to school, three kids were killed in car accidents. Not all of them in my class. They were drinking and got into car accidents, not unusual then and it still isn't.

▷ **Elaine, born in 1938**
grew up in the village of Botha, Alberta

Everything I remember about school was good. There was pressure. I guess it was more important then to, well, you used your marks, not only to please yourself but to be popular maybe. We had a very domineering principal. He didn't hesitate to use the strap. So he did a lot of teaching by threat. In grade ten math, we had thirty theorems and if we didn't memorize them perfectly, we were going to get the strap.

I can remember the catalogues that came up from the States. I got my graduation dress from there. When I graduated, there was only five of us. I quite impressed my kids for years telling them I was valedictorian of my graduating class and then they saw my graduation picture. When they graduated there was two hundred in their class. They called my bluff.

▷ **Dwayne, born in 1939**
grew up in Brandon, Manitoba

I went to Fleming School. In 1950 I was in grade six and my teacher was Betty Gibson. There's an elementary school here named after her. She was fairly worldly and well travelled. Her father was a missionary or something in South Africa and she had spent some time there. She came back to Canada and was teaching in Brandon. I remember that she used to tell stories—it didn't matter what the subject was, history or mathematics or anything, she'd always have stories to tell. More worldly stories about places she'd been, whether it was Cairo or deepest Africa or whatever. The kids would just lap it up like puppies.

Our desks were those where the top would tip up. The inkwell was on top, or there was a hole there but we didn't actually use it. In approximately grade three, I was probably one of the first students at Fleming that was allowed to use a ball-point pen. I remember it was quite messy, but they let me get away with it. By grade six, all of the students in our classroom used ball-point pens so the inkwells were long gone by that time.

Up to grade seven all my teachers were women. Grade eight we had a man and I had him for four years in a row. As he progressed, I progressed. He was an excellent teacher.

I remember getting TB x-rays starting in about grade five or so. As a kid you never knew what you were getting your shots for. You never knew and you didn't care. In Brandon, they did it every two years or so. We'd have the first shots in grade one, the second batch or boosters in grade three and then the next batch you got was grade six, and then you went to junior high and got your next batch over there. That was about the time they had the shot for polio but, of course, I didn't have to take that. I'd had polio. That was around grade seven, grade eight.

Dwayne and his 1950 grade six Brandon champs soccer team from Fleming Elementary School. Dwayne says, "The boy standing to the left of the Phys. Ed. teacher was originally from Switzerland, and came to school in grade three, not knowing a word of English but could play great soccer. His family moved here after the war."

One of the best pieces of advice that I ever got in my life was—and I tried to always follow it—was "do unto others as you would have them do unto you." And of course that was written on the ruler that you had on your desk all the time. A wooden ruler. And I can remember seeing that and thinking how I would like to live like that. I don't suppose I have, but I've always tried to.

▷ **Marilyn, born in 1940**
grew up at Lake Cowichan, British Columbia

I remember the only corporal punishment ever levied against me was a ruler on the knuckles when the teacher asked me if I was chewing gum. That was a no-no. I had it stuffed up into the corner of the back of my mouth and she came along and asked me to open my mouth so she could look. And there it was, of course. So she made me go put it in the wood stove that was at the back of the classroom and then I got whacked for telling a lie.

One of the clubs in high school that lots of the girls belonged to was Future Teachers Club. I don't know if they still have Future Teachers Clubs in schools but one was certainly developed when I was in high school. What a boring thought!

I can remember getting a half-day off school when King George died and I remember Newfoundland coming into Confederation because the IODE marked this occasion with a ceremony.

Everybody played hooky from school now and then. One day in grade twelve my girlfriend and I spent the afternoon in her backyard sunning ourselves. My dad asked me about it that night. You couldn't get away with anything in a small community like that.

My mother always threatened to put me in a boarding school, Queen Margaret's in Duncan, in particular, if I didn't behave. Especially in grade nine when she thought I was boy crazy she kind of held that out as a threat. When one day a letter came from Queen Margaret's, I thought for sure I was on my way.

I can remember there being "shotgun" weddings—living in a small town there seemed to be lots of them. I can remember the first "shotgun" wedding and agreeing with all of my classmates that yes, whisper, whisper, it must be "shotgun." I was probably in grade eight, so I would have been thirteen. I went home that night and asked my mom what a "shotgun" wedding was. When I was in grade ten, three of my classmates got married and had babies shortly thereafter. Some of the marriages lasted, and some of them didn't. There was no sex education in school. I probably got a little smattering of it from my mother but it was quite embarrassing for her to talk about. So she wouldn't have mentioned it more than she absolutely had to.

I remember magazines that had all of these love-confession stories. My grandmother, my mother's mother, lived with us for quite some time—for all my going-to-school years. I was asked one day to pick up a magazine for her at the store, something like *True Story* would do. There were two kinds of *True Story*, an adventure-type magazine and one that was romance stories and so on. I remember buying the one that she didn't want. I couldn't imagine that she wanted to read love stories.

In high school, I was trying to prepare for university. As a commerce major, I had to take what was called Health and Personal Development, or HPD, with the grade tens, for three years running. Associated with this was a job study that I did each year. One year I did one on a nurse, one year a teacher and the third year a secretary. Obviously, those were the jobs that were most easily available for women. I didn't think about doing one on a physicist or an accountant or a doctor. But four of the girls in our class, including me, went on to university.

▷ **Audrey H., born in 1941**
grew up on a farm near Strongfield in south-central Saskatchewan

I started school part way through the year as Mom taught me at home for the first five or six months. My first school day, Dad drove me in a cutter, pulled by our mare Daisy, over the snowy fields to Cherrydale, the country school he had attended. When spring came, I went to school by horse and buggy with a neighbour girl, Mary Lemon.

In the springtime, marbles were the order of the day. We raced out at recess to see who went first. You had to hit five holes and after you made the middle hole you could shoot at other marbles to keep them away from the middle. When it got warmer, we played Pum-Pum-Pullaway, Prisoner's Base and softball. With a registration of anywhere from nine to twelve students in grades one to eight, we had quite a mix for softball. In early spring, if the slough near the school froze over, we'd bring our skates to school. One winter the snowbanks were really high and the older students dug down and had a big snow house. They'd block the door so us younger ones couldn't get in so we often wondered what went on in there!

In winter, we'd take potatoes all scrubbed up and ready to bake, and at first recess put them on a rim just inside the old furnace so we could have a hot baked potato for lunch. As noon approached, you could smell the inviting aroma of baking potatoes.

School concerts were a big event in the school year. We would start learning our parts to plays, drills, carols and poems in early November. A week before the concert, our fathers would put up a stage in the small schoolroom so we could rehearse on it. The small cloakroom where we hung our outerwear was used as a dressing room for our excited and nervous group of young people. At all the Christmas concerts, whether they were at school or Sunday School, all of the kids got a candy bag. The bag contained home-made candy, nuts and possibly a Mandarin orange. We all looked forward to this aspect of the concerts.

In spite of our parents' protests, Cherrydale was closed in 1953 and we were off to the town school. We didn't usually get to town very often so this was a big event in our lives. Riding the school bus was exciting at first, but little grade one kids usually had a nap on the bus going home.

In the town school, the winter pastime was table tennis. Spring and summer we had volleyball, softball and football. In the spring there was always a "field meet." All the students from four towns and two or three country schools would meet at one town to compete in track and field events. There would be a big parade of all the schools, each one with a banner, to start the day. The day ended with ball games.

▷ **Steve, born in 1941 in Edmonton**
moved to Williams Lake, British Columbia, in 1953

When we moved to Williams Lake in 1953, there was a population of about two thousand. One saddle shop, a theatre, a Chinese restaurant. It was a distribution point to the north. I was in grade seven when we moved. At that time Edmonton had street cars, Williams Lake still had wooden sidewalks. I remember showing up in school in a suit and feeling like a freak.

In grade five in Edmonton, we had a male teacher, Mr. Driver, a college student fresh from the oilfields. He told magnificent stories about his jobs in the summer where he was tarring the pipes for the pipelines and how at the end of the day he'd jump up, grab the door-jamb, kick off his pants and they would stand up in the corner, they were so covered in tar.

He taught science which was wonderful. We had old buzzers and batteries and stuff that none of the women teachers seemed to know anything about, but Mr. Driver knew science. He understood what I was doing when I was drawing steam engines and he thought it was wonderful rather than silly. He taught us how to make electrical motors. I really liked him.

▷ **Maxine, born in 1942**
grew up in Gypsumville, Manitoba

I went to school very early, when I was five and a half. I started just after Christmas. That meant I went into grade two when I should have been going into grade one the next September. It meant that I was always the youngest in the class. Most of the other kids were farm kids and they didn't go to school until they were seven. Therefore, there was a real age gap.

The first school I went to was grades one to eight in one room and there probably would have been twenty students. There was a high school, grades nine to eleven with twelve or so students. When I went into grade three, they split the class into one to six and seven to eleven.

Really though, it was a two-room school until I got to grade six. Then we had three. There never was anymore than that.

I was the first girl to go to university from that area, in a radius of probably fifty miles. Most of the girls were pregnant and married by fourteen or fifteen, or married and pregnant, whichever order it came in. For girls, there was not a very bright future. It really wasn't. My father took a lot of ribbing for sending girls to university. It wasn't too bad the first time, but when he sent the second daughter, Well, was this man mad? He took a lot of flak.

▷ **Peter B., born in 1942 in England**
 came to Canada in 1944 and grew up in Regina, Saskatchewan

When I went to grade one, the school was about a mile and a half away. I walked, of course, and in winter had to walk over snowbanks and across the creek. I made a number of stops at homes my mom had arranged for me to check into, to get warm and to make sure I was okay. On the return trip, I'd stay longer at these homes, or at least at the ones who had children.

One time I was pretty late and my mother got worried. Knowing I'd get a licking when I got home, I avoided it as long as possible. My mother was English and was very strict, disciplining me to the point that, today, Social Services might intervene. So when I saw her waiting at the door as I approached, I decided to hightail it to the neighbour's in the pouring rain and mud. My father came after me and took me home. I got a good licking for running away.

▷ **Rupee, born in 1943 in India**
 came to Canada in 1947 and grew up in Victoria, British Columbia

I came to Canada with my family in 1947—from India by tramp steamer. It took us about three months to get here. It was fairly difficult the first two or three years because we didn't know the language. So when we got here, I had to learn the language in a hurry to start kindergarten. By kindergarten, I knew enough to get by. There were lots of kids around the neighbourhood. In the area that we lived in there were a number of families who were multicultural: Chinese, people from Poland, East Indians. There was a whole conglomeration of people. I got by okay in kindergarten but in grade one the language was catching up to me and I used to have to go upstairs to a room where there were lots of other children, Chinese and East Indian kids. I guess it was an ESL class. There were lots of fights—trying to find the pecking order in the school. We loved sports so we played every game that we could.

▷ **Bob, born in 1943**
grew up in Regina, Saskatchewan

I went to Connaught School on Thirteenth and Elphinstone. One teacher stands out in my mind. A teacher by the name of Miss B——, a kindergarten teacher. There was a boy in my class who I'm pretty sure had cerebral palsy. I was six at the time and I remember the teacher smacking his hands with a ruler because he couldn't print clearly. I remember getting up and screaming at her and telling her not to do that. I had no idea what his problem was but I just knew there was nothing he could do about it and she was wrong.

For high school, I went to Balfour Tech. My first girlfriend was Nora. I would've been twelve or thirteen, somewhere in there. I was madly in love with her and I remember she did allow me to kiss her once. It was sort of, "Well, if you have to."

▷ **John, born in 1943**
grew up in Winnipeg, Manitoba

I remember one incident from preschool. We went to a kindergarten, a German kindergarten, and it was run by a lady called Tanta Anna. Tanta is aunt in German. My recollection was that she was a mean lady. I remember going down the street—my mother was taking me there and I remember her getting a stick to make me go to kindergarten. I hated that whole kindergarten scene!

I went to public school from first grade through the seventh and then I went to a Mennonite high school—the Mennonite Brethren Collegiate Institute. It didn't feel like an odd thing to be there because we were all in the same boat. The guys you hung out with were the guys who went there, guys you saw in church. I think you got a good education although, at the time, I didn't particularly care about that.

The discipline was pretty strict. My brother, who was the rebel in the family, got kicked out of school for playing cards. The school was concerned with everything about you, including your spiritual life, so that meant that there was more rules than there would be in a regular school. They taught Mennonite history. And German used to be our

Mickey Mouse subject because we spoke it at home. We'd have to write the provincial exam so that was an easy one for us to pass.

The teacher who stands out in my mind is a guy we used to call J.R. and he was a very enthusiastic teacher. He taught poetry which didn't particularly interest us but he did it with enthusiasm. He was full of life. I gained a respect for poetry because if a teacher really appreciates it you tend not to write it off as easily. I met him once after I finished school and he said, "How are you?" and I said, "Fine." He said, "You're not fine, you're great!" He was that kind of a guy.

One day a week, every week, we went to German school. That was in the church basement. I tried to get out of being German. I grew up at a time when it wasn't very cool to be German. So I said to my mother, "Well, you were born in Russia, my dad was born in Russia and their parents were born in Russia and probably their parents were born in Russia." And she said, "Just because you were born in a barn doesn't mean you're a cow!"

▷ Lil, born in 1944
grew up in and near Nampa in northern Alberta

I remember one year we were all given little Bibles at school. But when we reached grade nine, we had to pass that Bible on to someone in a lower grade. I gave mine to George and years later he showed it to me, and when I opened it, I found the inscription I had written when I gave it to him: "Read it more than I did."

▷ Linda H., born in 1944
grew up on a farm near Marsden, Saskatchewan

I went to a country school, Wycollar School, until grade eight when the school closed and we were bused to town. In the country school there was probably about twenty-five kids and one poor teacher for all the grades from one to eight. The ones in grades nine and ten took correspondence and she supervised them too.

I loved school and couldn't wait to get there. In fact I started when I was five. We lived about a quarter of a mile from school and I would go and sit outside the school because my older family members were all there and there was nothing to do at home. I made a nuisance of myself so I was invited in if I would be quiet. The teacher started a kindergarten for me because I happened to be there and she liked me. The teacher lived in a teacherage, a little house right in the schoolyard.

Mostly we had women teachers.

The school was like a small hall with a big pot-bellied wood stove at the back. And the old traditional desks with the arm. I don't know what they were called. There were a few with a lifting lid and the whole row was attached. There were inkwells but we never used them. We had ink bottles and fountain pens that used to leak all over everything. Sometimes you'd open the bottle and forget to put the lid back on and get ink all over your lap.

At recess we went outside, even in winter, too. But we didn't seem to mind it. Day after day we played Fox and Goose, the game with the circles. It was a wonderful game. There was a dugout close by and on Friday afternoons we could go skating. We'd freeze water in cans and curl, too.

One of the things I always loved was we had a travelling library. Books would arrive in a big green box. I couldn't wait for that box to come. I can still remember the smell of it. Sometimes everything in it I'd want to read and other times there'd only be one or two. The rest would be non-fiction history books and who wanted to read those?

At the end of the day, we cleaned the boards and the brushes. The boys had to sweep the floor.

For grade nine, we started going to town school. It was a different culture. We were bused forty miles. On the bus at 6:30 a.m., dark and cold. It was hard the first year because I was shy and didn't know anybody. By grade ten, I loved it. Made good friends, got to know it wasn't cool to answer questions. Mostly it wasn't cool to act like you cared about school or were interested. I always had been, so this was real weird but I could learn to fit in. It was more important to fit in than it was to make it in school. We used to sneak out at recess—five or six of us would hang out outside the pool hall. The boys could go in but not the girls.

Later in high school, some girls disappeared to go away to high school. Others had to get married.

▷ **JoAnne, born in 1944**
grew up in Dawson City, Yukon

My first day of school was kind of scary, as I recall. I remember not being too anxious to go that day. Because my parents were in business, my mother went to Vancouver on buying trips. Her father lived in Vancouver so we went and spent part of the summer with him. It was the year that I was to start school. I really did not want to go to school and when people talked to me about it, I insisted that I was not going. My mother took us to wholesale warehouses where she was doing some buying. The sales representatives would tell me that if I would go to school, they would give me a book or some other wonderful present. I took all the bribes, but was still determined that I was not going to go to school. However, when fall came, I ended up going to school just like everyone else, and actually, it wasn't a bad experience when I got there. The school was a two-storey building that had been built in the 1900s and that's the school we went to until it burned down in June of 1957. Because the school burned and we didn't have any other place to go, that fall we went to school in what was then the Yukon Government Administration Building. The capital had moved from Dawson City to Whitehorse and this building was then left partially vacant. A lot of us went to school there, for a year and a half, until they built a new school. It opened in January 1959. When we moved in it was sixty-four degrees below zero.

Souvenir Coronation cup and saucer.

I remember the Coronation. I have my souvenir coin and the book that was published that year. A little red book. I have it. And I have my flag. I also remember John Diefenbaker coming to Dawson City in 1958. It was a big event. We got his autograph.

I got the strap a couple of times. Earned it once. The second time I didn't. That time I was just passing a note that somebody passed to me to pass to somebody else and I got caught with it. Of course you wouldn't squeal on anybody either, so I was taken into the cloakroom and I got five strokes on the hand with a leather strap. Of course, if you got it at school, you got it again at home too.

I went to boarding school in Victoria for grade eleven and then back to Dawson for grade twelve. There was only about six of us in the graduating class. Many had moved away. There just weren't jobs. Economically, it wasn't a very prosperous time.

The year that I went to St. Ann's Academy in Victoria for grade eleven, it struck me as strange that most of the students there were from all around BC and some were even from the States. I remember being very intimidated when I got there because I thought these kids would know so much more than I did because they had been more exposed to news and everything. But I was surprised to find out that I knew a lot more about them and their environment than they did about us and our environment. They had no idea how I even got from Dawson to Whitehorse to Vancouver. They thought I lived in an igloo and ate blubber and travelled by dogsled. I couldn't believe that. It really struck me as strange. I remember being in a Social Studies class and we were talking about the north and I couldn't believe what they were saying! I phoned my father and asked him to send me some slides so I could show them that's not how we live. So I showed the slides and gave a little talk about what it was like to live in the north.

▷ **Dennice, born in 1944**
grew up on a farm near Dodsland, Saskatchewan

I remember my first day of school. That was a very big deal, of course. The afternoon or the night before my first day of school, I remember having my hair washed and put up in metal curlers and being talked to at length about never telling any stories at school about what went on at home.

I went to public school in the country with grades one to eight there. There were a number of boys who were older and I remember one of them in particular who had his driver's licence. There always seemed to be lots of older kids putting the younger kids together, boy and girl, in a cutter. And picking on certain kids. I remember one day some of the older boys were hiding from the teacher up in the attic. They were also taking the little kids and hanging them on hooks three-quarters of the way up the wall in the cloakroom by their belts.

Probably the biggest event during the school year was the Christmas concert. I think the teacher was judged by the community on the quality of the concert she could put on. There would be a certain number of drills, songs, plays and recitations. They would put those same benches crosswise in front of the stage and hang green curtains around the stage. After the Christmas concert was over, Santa Claus would come and every child would get a bag of candy with peanuts and an orange. There were two occasions during the year when you had to lay down right after lunch to have a sleep and one of those days was the day of the Christmas concert. Of course you never slept, because you were very excited.

Dennice and her classmates at the country school, 1954.

Our whole life revolved around the school when I was young. My mom used to tell the story about going to these schoolhouse dances in the early forties before they had a vehicle. Dad's horses were young and frisky and he'd hook them up to the sleigh or cutter and circle the house while Mom would throw one child at a time into the sleigh. The horses were just too rambunctious to bring to a complete halt.

I remember as a very young child going to the school dances. They used to play whist, a card game, before the dancing started and then they'd have lunch. People would bring sandwiches in cookie tins. The men would go to the basement and make coffee in a big double boiler, and they'd stir it with an axe handle. After lunch there would be a dance and the kids would go to sleep under the benches. Local people would provide the music. There'd be a piano player, because there was always a piano in the school, and an accordion and a fiddle. Maybe a banjo. Later on when I was in grade seven or eight, I was aware that at lunch time—this would be when people had cars—at lunch time the young people would all go out to their cars. I can remember asking my mother what they were doing out in the cars.

At the dances they would play a combination of old and new music. Songs like "Mary Ann," "Marie" and the "Blue Skirt Waltz." At the country dances there was a variety of polkas, fox trots and schottisches. And then there was a round dance. Later at the town dances there were those and jiving and the butterfly. I remember when it was important to have a pair of nylons for the dance, and it wasn't unusual if the husbands would be in town and that they would pick up a pair of nylons for their wives. Of course this was when you wore nylons, the ones with the seam up the back.

At the country dances the women would all be seated on one side and the men would be on the other. When the music started the men would go across the floor to ask a woman to dance. You would dance to one song and then the music would stop and you'd walk around with your partner until the music started again and then you'd start to dance again. After three songs, they'd play a little ditty and that would signal the end of the set and you'd sit down ready to dance with another partner. If you were dancing with someone you didn't like, you'd think the end of the third song would never come. If you were dancing with someone you liked, the third song came far too soon.

Every July 1, there was a sports day. There would be ball games all day long. There would be a supper and then a dance that night. We always had a picnic at the end of school term at the country school. The people would play ball and different ball teams would come from all over. These weren't school-age ball teams. They would be adult ball teams. There would be tables outside the school of planks set up on sawhorses, and they would sell pop from buckets filled with ice. I think there were chocolate bars and home-made things. And ice cream and watermelon. That's what I remember. That would be the first time in the year that you got watermelon and they would cut these huge pieces. And then there would be a supper at night and people would eat outside. They would have brought potato salad, cold meats, jellied salads and pickles.

▷ **Giuliana (Julia), born in 1944 in Italy**
   came to Canada in 1953 and grew up in Michel, British Columbia

I took all my schooling in Italy—my communion, my confirmation, everything. At age eleven, I would have been in grade nine in Italy. Here, they put me in grade six. I had to learn everything. It was hard. I didn't know English. But most of the kids were Italian and they helped. They were really, really good. But when you had Italian parents and everybody else was Italian, it was very hard to learn English. So bang, you were put in a grade. And you had to learn.

The majority of my teachers were men. Actually, our present dentist in Calgary, his brother used to be the principal of the school. The one who became a dentist used to work in the mines with my dad to put himself through school.

I went to high school in Sparwood, by bus. I started high school in about 1956. I did a couple of years of high school.

▷ **Ed, born in 1946**
grew up in Saskatoon, Saskatchewan

In school, I was a bit of a misfit. I wasn't interested in sports and those kind of things. I think I was reasonably bright and I liked writing, but I didn't fit into the traditional male activities. Plus I was in for several eye operations—I had eye problems all the way along so I was probably what my son would call a geek. I used to read a tremendous amount. I was the kind of kid who, when we studied things, would go to the library and read about it. I read about how to make gun powder and how to make explosives, bombs and all of those kind of things. In many ways, school provided the opportunity to start on things and then I'd read about them. School was a minor part of my life, more of a stepping stone.

I remember all my teachers. Several pushed me to discover and develop my interest in writing. One teacher was a nun. Another teacher was a real battle axe, but liked two or three of us. When I was in grade eight our teacher was this great big man who I actually ended up working with later on the school board and when he was a deputy minister. He intimidated us so much that when offered the choice to return to the battle axe's classroom because his was full, we jumped at the chance. From then on we were diamonds in her eyes!

I went to a Catholic elementary school and a Catholic high school. In kindergarten, grade one and grade six the teachers were nuns. I think that, from a woman's point of view, becoming a teacher was much the same then as it is now. The first-year teachers or the ones who were fairly new were single, as they are now, and the older ones—I had a couple who were maybe thirty or forty—seemed like they were as old as the hills, they were married. The city, of course, always seemed to get the plums. So there were far fewer of the one-year wonders, mainly because the city could afford to pay more and the opportunities were greater in a city. It would have been much more difficult to get a job in the city with only one year of Normal School and no experience.

In high school, of course, I had mostly male teachers. I went to a segregated all-boys high school and there were many priests. In high school I got into electronics in a big way. In grade eleven, I got my ham radio licence and chatted to people all over the world.

We got TB x-rays every year. Even right up to college. When I first went to university, I remember clearly they'd park the van right up by the old Administration Building and parade everybody through it, especially the teachers.

▷ **Gail, born in 1946**
grew up in Prince Rupert, British Columbia

The first male teacher I had was in grade five. Male teachers were quite unusual, and my friends and I decided that this was going to be terrible. A man teacher! And he wasn't a young man. I recall now, he probably wasn't as old as I thought he was, probably forty-five or fifty but he seemed like an older guy. We thought we'd have to quit school or something. It was quite different, more structured, and he wanted us to call him "sir" which we did. In actual fact, it wasn't a bad thing at all. There were rules and you followed them. It wasn't that tough for us.

Our school in Prince Rupert was an old frame building. The girls had their playground on one side of the school and the boys had theirs on the other. We came in through separate doors and lined up to go in.

Mr. Freeman, our grade-five teacher, taught the girls a bouncing ball routine. You remember how everyone played with those hard India rubber balls, lacrosse balls? We had a group of ten or so girls. We wore white T-shirts and short white skirts that our mothers made for us and we had these routines with songs that went with them.

There was a big deal made about the Coronation. Something took place in Prince Rupert down on the wharf. It must have been when a ship was in. We all went down to the wharf. There was a festive atmosphere.

In school, it seemed everyone eventually got the strap. Although, as I never did, I guess everyone didn't, but my memories of the strap are very vivid. There was much talk about how to minimize the pain, whether you were supposed to lick your hands or you weren't to lick them. Should you hold your hands stiff or not? It was only on the hands and a quick whack. I wonder if anyone saved one.

▷ **Sandy, born in 1946**
grew up in Winnipeg, Manitoba

I remember Miss Ferguson, a young Scottish woman. At the end of grade one she got married and I was heartbroken because she wasn't going to be my teacher any more. I was jealous, I think.

My teacher in grade three was Miss V——. She was an unmarried lady, extremely tall and quite bony. Very into teaching. Bright red lipstick and fairly tight-fitting long skirts. She was very firm, yet she was quite kind and I liked her. Grade five was another Miss and she had dedicated her whole life to teaching and to her students. I was completely devoted to her and I thought she was the most wonderful person. She had quite dark hair with curls in it and she looked really distinguished. Very small build. That was the year I discovered I could write poetry. I cried every day because I couldn't do arithmetic and she would keep me after four and try and help me and I thought I was such a blockhead about it. She really encouraged my poetry. She had me read one of my poems in front of assembly. It was called "Where Do The Ships Go On The Sea?" and "Do they go to Zanzibar?" and all these places. That was quite a highlight.

In grade six, I had a teacher who was the bane of my life. He made me cry. He was mean and he used to throw things at me. One time I was reading my book and he was talking and I was supposed to be listening. He threw a book at me! Anyway, it turned out later that he got fired. For reasons that, I guess, had to do with him having little boys up on his knee. We didn't think anything of it at the time.

I remember not liking recess very much. There were a lot of organized games and things that I really didn't feel part of. As I look back, I don't remember one tree on the playground, just this feeling of being terribly exposed. When I went to play at home, I went to a huge field, a complete wilderness behind our place. I'd go and play there by the hour, happily tucked away among those bushes. By myself. Just this feeling of being completely hidden away. On the playground I felt there was nowhere to hide from anything.

I remember, after lunch, in the warm afternoons, listening to art class on the radio from Winnipeg and doing things according to what they said on the program.

I went into grade eight in this giant school, modern, one-level plate glass that seemed to go on forever. Extremely sterile. I thought it was just huge. I went there from grade eight and stayed there until grade twelve. We wore tunics, at least for grades eight, nine, ten. Everybody wore them, so we thought nothing of it. We wore them right through elementary too. They were navy with pleats and a woven-cord black belt that you tied at the side. You could wear black leotards. I think other than that we could wear what we wanted. Come grade eight, the girls had them all hooped and humped. They didn't look so neat any more.

In high school, my French teacher's name was Doc McCullough. He had white hair and he wore dark glasses. He had retired before and come back. He was a doctor of philosophy, a very free spirit and he had travelled all over the world. He played the ukulele. He used to say, "Okay class, get your French books out in case the principal comes in.

With some of her classmates in 1958, Sandy sits far right, in typical fifties garb including poodle skirt and neckerchief.

Now, I'll sing you a song about Flin Flon Flossie." He would talk about climbing the Alps and he would make really funny jokes. A total humanitarian. Once, we had him over for supper and when shortly after my father donated money to the football team he was starting, I started getting really good marks! I don't remember learning much French. In fact, I failed it when I got into the next class, and after I went to summer school, I started doing really well and went on to take Honours French. I joined the French Club and ended up going to Quebec. I really got into French. However, I learned something from Doc McCullough much more important than French. I learned not to worry about the principal, he didn't know where it was at.

As for sex education, I remember these very neat, little square booklets, like CD covers now. It was all about you and what happens to your body growing up. *Especially For You,* I think it was called. And then we had a film that the boys didn't see. I brought those booklets home and I remember hiding them in my drawer.

The only news event from the fifties that I remember was the formation of Ghana. I did a Social Studies project on it.

▷ **Candace, born in 1946**
  grew up in Edmonton, Alberta

I went to the same school from grade one right to grade nine. The thing I remember most about elementary school was on winter days kids would stick their tongues to the metal fence. The teacher would come out with a kettle and unstick this row of kids from the fence.

I liked going to school. I liked recess. I had lots of friends. I liked my teachers. I think I was just one of those normal kids who went to school. I grew up in a stable environment. We lived in the same house, didn't move around. Moved once when I was thirteen or fourteen and the next house we were there until I left home. I went to the same school so I had the same friends throughout school. The thing that I found difficult was I had a good friend in grade one and she moved away. She was my best friend and to this day I don't know where she is. Another really good friend when I was in junior high—she got pregnant, she was fifteen or sixteen, and she got married and went away and I never saw her again either. It's really sad. People that you really cared about. Just gone.

▷ **Ken, born in 1947 in Victoria**
grew up just outside Edmonton, Alberta

I was an honour student all the way through. School was a lot stricter then, but I got away with a lot because of my marks. We had a pretty high drop-out rate, although you've got to remember you're looking at the oilfield and the pipeline being built then. So a kid could leave school at grade eight or grade nine and could get a $2-an-hour job. That was big bucks in those days.

▷ **Louise, born in 1947**
grew up in Slocan, British Columbia

I remember the first teacher I had, Mrs. F——. She had two little boys. One of them had something, a disease, that he died from. The other one had polio and he eventually died too. She didn't have a husband, or I don't remember him anyway. We had heard that he had passed away. There was another boy in school about my brother's age who got polio and survived, but he had a limp after that.

There were grades one to six in the school. About sixty kids and three teachers. There was a cloakroom where you put your mitts and hats and you hung your coats on hooks. There were blackboards and library shelves and tables at the back where you did your artwork. The desks were metal with wood fronts and wood seats. They were hooked together on runners and you could flip the seat up. They had inkwells that we actually used. We used those red straight pens.

In school, when you wanted to go to the bathroom, you had to put up your hand and say whether you had to go number one or number two. When I first started school we had an outhouse. There was the girl's side and the boy's side and boys would always be trying to look in the girl's side.

There were Japanese kids in the school, kids whose parents had been in the internment camps. We didn't really know anything about what happened. When you're kids you don't really realize that there's a problem. A lot of the Japanese worked at my dad's sawmill so it wasn't any big deal that you had Japanese kids you went to school with. They were no different than you were.

It was scary going from grade six to grade seven because that's when you went to high school. Junior high and high school were the same. I never liked school. There was other things I'd rather be doing, like being at home, cooking and baking. The teachers would tell me that I was quite rebellious. I remember one teacher I had who was very religious. If she thought that you didn't believe in Jesus or God, then she had it in for you. I can remember getting hit on the top of the head with the corner of a reader or math book. I jumped up out of my desk and she said, "The devil's got you, the devil's got you!" Little did she know, it probably had her.

▷ **Greg, born in 1947**
grew up on the Tsartlip Reserve on Vancouver Island, British Columbia

We had an Indian school, Tsartlip Indian School. I went there for six years, went up to grade six. We had prayers every morning and at lunch time. Every morning we'd line up on the patio and sing "O Canada." My first-grade teacher was Sister Daniels. She was short. We had a lot of respect for her—in those days we had a lot of respect for priests and nuns. She didn't really favour anybody and it seemed as though she cared about all of us. I remember one day I got into trouble. She stood me up in front of the class and said, "Okay, you're going to discipline yourself. Here's a ruler." She gave me a ruler. "And you're going to whack your hand." She wasn't angry so I didn't really believe her, but I whacked my hand and broke the ruler. The class roared. She roared. She said, "You can sit down." And there was this ruler, a little splinter in my hand.

The nuns had a way of teaching discipline, you know the prayers, that really sort of kept us under control. We weren't angels. There was a certain degree of behaviour and conduct that they taught us. We took a lot for granted. We thought they'd always be there—the innocence of being in school and being looked after by the teachers and some of the visitors to the school. Just people that cared about students. There was two non-native elderly people, Mr. and Mrs. Hardy. They would come to the classroom, say, "Good morning," then pass out candies. We thought the world of them. Whoever they were. And we had a lot of respect for them. Not just because they brought candy. They cared about us.

One of the priests, Father Bradley, used to walk from Esquimalt. Someone would say, "Father Bradley's coming." We'd all automatically run out to meet him. We weren't given permission. You weren't allowed to leave the classroom but when Father Bradley came, we just all took off. He was a very gentle old priest. He was very soft-spoken. He was well respected not only here but in Victoria and district, but we thought he was our priest because he walked out to see us. If one of the kids asked him a question, he would answer. He respected us.

After grade six, I went to Mt. Douglas High School. We didn't have too much respect for most of the teachers. They didn't have too much respect for us. There were some teachers we respected. Some of them had a sense of humour, were very lenient. But we took it all in stride. I remember there was an initiation process and older students were bound and determined that they were going to initiate us. We wouldn't allow it. The students being initiated had to roll up their pant legs, slick down their hair and put on make-up. We were walking through the schoolyard, about six of us, and a group of big guys said they were going to prove they could initiate us. We said the native students would not allow themselves to be initiated. It ended up about ten of them fighting us and the rest of them backed off. We made an impression and I think we got a certain amount of respect after that. We started to adjust, join in the games and we realized some of the non-native females were attracted to us. We were a part of the school but not a big part. I was there two years. Then I went to residential school for grades nine and ten. It was terrible.

▷ **Thelma, born in 1948**
grew up in Vancouver in British Columbia

I was lucky enough that when I started school the system didn't force me to change from left-handed to right. Mother told me Mr. Houston, the principal, had a psychologist brother who believed that forcing right-handedness caused problems. Only trouble was the Maclean

Method of handwriting made no provision for back-slanted writing. Does anyone else remember painful hours of writing ovals? You were supposed to use your arm muscle as a little swivel to swing your arm on. The whole exercise was painful to both me and my teacher.

I have a clear memory of the first day of school, standing in a long line of mothers and children in the "girls' basement." There seemed to be a long delay, perhaps due to my excitement, but possibly because there were too many kids. Consequently, after a couple of days another teacher was brought in, and I left Miss Galliford's room for Miss Burdett's. The room had six rows of desks, each bolted to runners. The seat of one was connected to the writing portion of the following. Thus there was a seat portion extra at the front of the row, a handy place for piles of texts, or the naughty kids. Phonics was strictly taught, as a reading method, and I still feel it is a good method. We really learned how to spell. I loved school but was absent sometimes because I made myself sick over unfinished work.

Perhaps the seed of the rebellious sixties was sown in the classrooms of the fifties. I especially remember Mr. McRae, the vice-principal, and Miss Burnham, my grade-six teacher, having a heated discussion about a fine point of grammar, right in front of the class. And on parents' day, when mothers and a few fathers were present, a boy stood up and openly disputed the teacher's statement that life on other planets was not possible. He said, "Why can't life be supported without oxygen?"

One day in high school the whole student body stayed outside after the afternoon bell. One of the girls had been sent home because her skirt was too short. Her knees were showing. Never mind that it was a short pleated skirt, and she had socks to just below her knees! So we went on strike until threatened with the police!

In general, though, classrooms were very quiet places. You put up your hand and asked for permission to leave the room. One teacher even required that if you had to use the bathroom during class, you stayed after school to make up time. With forty-two students in the average class, nice straight rows and rigid discipline must have been essential. Of course, there were those who acted up and the strap in the principal's office was a real threat.

On rainy days, of which there seems to have been many, we stayed in the basement at recess strictly separated by gender. Then the older girls sometimes led us in quiet games. I can't remember the name for one where we held hands and wound up like a snail shell. Another was Go-Go-Stop. "What time is it Mr. Wolf?" was another. Even in the playground, the boys had their area and the girls, another. We played a lot of hopscotch, tag, statues, "movie stars" and skipping games. When we got to grade five or six, baseball was very popular. Certain fields were the established property of certain classes, but we didn't pick sides. We played scrub.

I remember when the Queen was crowned and the television coverage, which was nearly the first TV I ever saw. Even that was not on our own set. The newspaper had a contest for kids to make scrapbooks of the Coronation. One of the girls from my school won an award. Her book was beautifully done, with each photo framed by a hand-drawn crown. It seems to me this girl's name was Beth—perhaps she was even named for the Queen.

Our school seems to have been almost all WASP. Maybe those who weren't English, Irish or Scottish didn't admit it. After all there was still a lot of postwar sentiment around. My immediate neighbourhood was a few short blocks of dead-end streets sandwiched between a major road, a golf course and an Indian Reserve. The Indian children went to residential school, and were only later admitted to the public school system. As for other visible minorities, there were almost none. A Japanese family moved in up the street and I'm ashamed to say I believed what the other children said about them being our enemy. I know I didn't hear that kind of talk in my home, where acceptance was the rule.

▷ **Karen, born in 1949**
   grew up in Victoria, British Columbia

When I was in grade one or two, the Victoria School District hired its first speech/language pathologist. But that was once a week for twenty minutes for me. And I had the same person for twelve years. We finally had it out the fall of my last year in high school. She was very structured, a rigid type of personality.

I went to Quadra Elementary. The academic part was hard, and I put up with a lot of everyday abuse at school. I had chalk thrown at me and had my hand cut by a teacher once, to get my attention, because I was deaf and wasn't responding. I was writing in my notebook. The next day was probably the only day that my dad broke his routine and didn't get on the bus to go to work. He walked to school with me and talked to the principal.

There was a real push to get my brother and I out of the school system. We were referred to as deaf and dumb or the deaf mutes in the

school. But my dad was persistent. One year he was the only man going to the PTA meetings. Back then men didn't usually attend PTA,
just women.

There were lots of things that weren't very pleasant on the academic side but, on the other hand, I really loved sports so I was very
much involved with that part of school and a lot of the mischievous
things that happened there. I didn't see myself different in that way. I
don't remember a lot of problems with my peers other than what I
would consider the normal competition that you would find anywhere.

In grade four I happened to be in the class of one of Victoria's
prominent choir conductors and she was a teacher. She was determined
to win all of the contests with that choir. I couldn't sing worth a darn,
still can't, so she used to bribe me to stand at the back of the choir and
mouth the words.

▷ **Anne, born in 1949 in Winnipeg**
grew up in Calgary, Winnipeg, Vancouver, Victoria and Edmonton

In grade four, we had a female teacher, a very large, imposing, buxom
figure who demanded strict discipline from the class because they were
such big classes. If you had forty in a class, it was nothing. My grade-
five teacher was an Englishman, again another strict disciplinarian, and
I remember one little incident when he admonished me for yawning in
class without putting my hand in front of my mouth. I didn't know
you were supposed to do that. A little piece of etiquette that I guess I
missed at home. I was mortified. I'd committed a social *faux pas* in
front of the class and he admonished me!

I did very well academically, although for my father it was never
enough. I would come home with ninety-nine percent and the first
remark would not be "Good for you, isn't that great?" It would be
"Where did the one percent go?" But it was always done in sort of a
jocular manner so you could never call him on it. No matter how well
you did, it was never good enough.

▷ **Linda C., born in 1949**
grew up in Calgary and Sylvan Lake, Alberta

I remember arriving on the first day of school and there were so many
of us, they didn't know what to do. They sent us all home until they
could hire some more teachers and set up some classrooms. We were at

home for a couple of days until they could get their act together.

Starting in about grade five, there were little book clubs. They probably still do that at schools, where you sell books and if you sell so many you get so many. So I used to like to sell a lot so that I could get a lot. Another memory I have of being a child which was kind of funny —because I was Catholic, I couldn't be a Brownie. Back then you couldn't belong to non-church groups. One of the biggest disappointments of my life was not being able to go out and sell Brownie cookies. I thought that was the cat's meow to be able to go door-to-door to sell to people because you could meet all these people. Even as a six year old, I wanted to go out and sell Brownie cookies. Being able to sell the books was a big deal to me.

I remember my grade-one teacher having a cookie sheet and she put this jelly-like substance on it and would somehow trace lines into it. Then she'd individually put sheets of paper on it and rub them and that would photocopy whatever was on it. That was even prior to the old Gestetner. Schoolteachers have come a long way since then.

In school you didn't step out of line, that's for sure. Certain boys would always act out, typically the farm boys, and were always getting into a bit of mischief. The way the school was lined up, the smart kids were in rows one and two, the medium kids in three and four and then the dumb kids were in row five. If you went from row one to row two, you started wondering if your marks were going down hill. The bad kids were put in the front of whichever row they happened to be in so they were closer to the teacher. It was always important for me to sit in the back of row one.

We had the kind of desk with the square sliding boxes underneath your seat where you kept everything. And it had a wrap-around arm with a little groove at the top for your pen and an inkwell. I used an inkwell in grade one with a straight-edge pen, but by about grade two or three the ball-point pen had come in and we were allowed to use them. When you got into grade four or five, then you got the desk where the desk became the seat of the one in front of it. About then, stirrup pants were in style but you had to have a crease in them. Very important or they used to bag at the knees something awful. So girls would always sit with their legs very straight so that they wouldn't get the baggy knees. Sometimes somebody would come and sit down. Because you'd wedged your feet up underneath the seat they'd sit down and just about break your toes.

In Bowness we had to wear skirts but in Sylvan Lake we could wear slacks in school. They were a little more lax, especially because I had about a mile to walk to school.

For the first few grades I had a lunch box with some kind of design on it. I think I had a Roy Rogers one year. Then I took just a brown paper bag. It wasn't cool by grade four or five to have a lunch box. I remember I always had a sandwich and a half made of white bread. My favourite was Velveeta cheese and bologna with salad dressing on it. And two cookies and an apple. That was lunch absolutely every day.

I remember getting a prize for having the best handwriting in grade five. Somebody sent me a cheque for a buck or something for winning this handwriting prize. I kept it for years. I was so proud of my handwriting. I was told I had teacher's handwriting. It's slipped a bit now but it's still legible at least. We concentrated on writing pages and pages of just the letter A perfectly. Writing that B just perfectly. Closing your O's. We spent hours practising that. It was very important because, in handwriting, you got the best stars. Gold stars were the best, silver was for second best and then red was "you're okay." We wanted to get lots of stars.

As I got older several teachers stood out. Our math teacher—he was an excellent teacher—was black. It was very unusual to have any black teachers. My French teacher stands out in my mind because he was a drunk. He used to play these little films in class and day after day we'd see the same film with the same little bouncing ball. I just didn't have any respect for him so I was a bit lippy by the time I got to grade eleven or twelve and I got myself into trouble. He finally expelled me. Of course I needed French to graduate from high school so I got a week's detention. Never got the strap though. Mostly boys got the strap.

In grade seven they had a really hard time getting and keeping teachers. I mean, that's a bad age to teach anyway. I was in a grade seven-eight split of girls and there was a seven-eight split of boys. I think the boys' class in particular was hard to handle. The teacher we ended up with came out of retirement and she wore all these really, really old-fashioned clothes. At the time we thought she was out-to-lunch so we gave her a hard time.

Discipline meant being kept in after school. The vice-principal had the detention room and you didn't want to mess with him. We really did get taught how to act. At one school gymnasium forum we had some performers and I remember a couple of kids got up and walked across the front of the stage. The next day, they called the whole school in. The vice-principal reamed everybody out for poor manners—that you don't walk in front of the stage, you don't get up until it's intermission—and he went through all the things you're allowed and not allowed to do.

I was always an extremely good student. Being good academically was very much stressed in our house. We were rewarded at report card time. If you got an A you got ten cents, and if you got a B you got five cents and Cs were failures as far as my parents were concerned—and as far as I was concerned, even though C is an average grade. You definitely didn't want anything less than a B.

Both my parents had a grade-eight education. That was as far as they could go. There was no school after that. I think that was part of the prairie values, people came over and realized that to have their children go further than they did, they needed a good education. I think my mother always wanted to be a schoolteacher and I thought that I was going to live out that dream, especially since I was the oldest. And I did.

I remember a couple of girls in grade nine leaving school suddenly to go and live with their aunts for a period of time. It wasn't talked about openly.

We had a graduating class of twelve—six matriculated and the other six just took diplomas. Not many went very far with their education. There was a boy in school I considered a bit of a geek. The brightest boy in class. He was my competition. He went on to do a Master's degree in computer science. I'm sure he's got a very, very good job somewhere.

▷ **Dennis, born in 1949**
grew up in Burnaby, British Columbia

I was a child of the Catholic school system. The school was at least two miles from home so I had to take the bus every day. So there I was, a six-year-old kid going on the bus, all by myself. Today, in Vancouver, that would be totally unheard of. You don't put a six-year-old kid on a bus and send them off to school. If I felt like it and the weather was good, I would walk home. It was no big deal. We didn't think anything of it.

The majority of the kids all lived within the immediate neighbourhood in north Burnaby, where the school was, but I, and a few others, lived farther away. During the day, I'd go to school with kids that lived in one part of that neighbourhood and in the evening I'd be at home and going out and playing with kids who went to a totally different school. That led to very strained and unusual approaches to life. Years later I realized that I had been discriminated against. I was different because I didn't go to school with them. I was bullied, called names, taunted.

One thing I remember, because of Sputnik in 1958, my class, my age group in school, was always the first ones to get the new curriculum. The kids that were ahead of us in the next class, they'd get the books that were in the schools for the last twenty years, the old curriculum. We got all the new stuff, the new books. I've always wondered how that may have affected learning over the years. We were the guinea pigs, the first ones that were told, "You have to learn French." We were the ones that were told, "It is no longer arithmetic, you've got to do math. It's no longer science, you've got to learn biology." It was interesting. Of course we attribute that to Sputnik in 1958. That was the push. We certainly weren't hurt by it, that's for sure.

▷ **Dan, born in 1949**
  grew up on a ranch near Lundbreck in southern Alberta

I went to kindergarten in Fort Macleod. My second-grade teacher was a super person. All of my teachers were female up to grade seven. My wife and I went to school together, we met in grade one. I went to high school at Black Diamond. It was a brand new school, Oilfields High School.

▷ **George, born in 1950**
  grew up in Vanderhoof and Prince George, British Columbia

I remember I really didn't like starting school. The year before, they had built a new school right behind the row of houses we lived in. It was just a two-room school that housed grades one to four. The next year they added an annex for grades five and six. Starting school meant taking me away from my mother. She started working full time then, so after school and for lunch, we had to go to a neighbour's house. I really missed my mom. In grade one I had to stay after school to practise my printing, and after the teacher had checked my work, I got smacked across the fingers with the edge of a ruler because it wasn't quite up to her expectations. In grade two, I got the strap for picking on a kid, actually just teasing him along with everyone else because of his new haircut. He really had it coming because he was a real little bully and always teasing others until they cried. I really didn't think that was fair either. Maybe his antics were ignored because he was related to the principal, I don't know. That strap really stung and I thought it was unfair.

▷ **Bruce, born in 1950**
  grew up in Winnipeg, Edmonton and Regina

Starting school was pretty exciting. I learned to read with the Dick and Jane readers. I remember playing tag on the school grounds. Marbles. I remember fighting with the other boys. There were schoolyard bullies, that has not changed. I remember loving reading. Anything to do with reading. There was a lot of testing and they always sent notes home that said, according to the tests, I should be doing much better and I spend too much time talking. My mother used to go to school and say, "Well, don't you understand, he's a bright kid and you're boring him?" My mom was an exceptional woman who would stand up to any teacher. They didn't always like what she had to say and she was pretty formidable.

While in school we got regular x-rays for TB and booster shots every few years. Polio was a big one. And that one really hit home because one of my cousins got polio in the big epidemic in Winnipeg in '54 or '55. You could see whenever they came to visit he had a shrivelled left arm. I can remember discussing it with the family and Mom would say, "Well, that's why you have to have your shots."

When we went camping in the summer on the south shore of Lake Winnipeg, there were still quite a few aboriginal families around at the time. They were still hunting and trapping and fishing. I certainly remember them there but not in the neighbourhood or in the city. I do remember people from Germany and Holland moving into the neighbourhood. A lot of Dutch and German immigrants in the fifties. By the time I started school we had moved to another neighbourhood, a working-class district off St. Mary's Road, St. Vitale, in Winnipeg. That was a little more varied: some Ukrainian kids, Icelanders, Scots.

▷ **Audrey R., born in 1953**
  grew up on a farm near Pelly, Saskatchewan

I went to a one-room country school from grade one to grade four. There were grades one to nine in that single room, about sixteen of us

*Audrey and her classmates inside the country school
she attended. It's 1961 and Audrey's in grade three.
At this time, the school did not have electricity.*

in most years. The teacher
was a married woman with
three older kids. School
was about two and a half
miles from home and the
teacher would drive around
picking us all up on the
way to school. In the wintertime a couple of older
kids got paid monthly to go
to school early and light
the furnace. They got $2
or $3 a month. The teacher
brought water every day to
fill the ceramic crock. It
had a tap on it and that was
our drinking water. We each had our own enamel mug. That was ours
as long as we were in school. Until I was in grade four, there was no
electricity in the school.

The teacher always wore a dress. In fact when there was a blizzard
she used to take us to school with a team and sleigh. And I can remember her son helping her get into the sleigh which was difficult because
she had a tight skirt on, down below her knees. He practically had to
pick her up and throw her over the side of the grain box. She always
wore a dress. The only time she wore slacks was once a year at the school
picnic.

We took a lunch to school, of course. My favourite was salmon
sandwiches and an apple. We had that three or four times a week. In
the summer we rode horses to school and sometimes our bicycles. We
played ball in the summer and Fox and Geese in the wintertime. We
had snowball fights, planned snowball fights, always girls against the
boys. And we built snow forts. The schoolyard was huge, so in the
summer we could go back in the bush and build a fort. There would be
a girls' fort and a boys' fort. We built our fort well enough that often
from inside we couldn't hear the school bell. I don't know what the
boys' fort looked like inside because, of course, girls weren't allowed.

Having fun and being cool

As children in the early fifties, we made our own fun, playing fantasy games—games fuelled by our limited experience—and by radio, picture shows, comics and books. Theatres showed regular Saturday matinees that featured a kiddies cartoon and one or two serial movies. Some of our fondest memories of being children in the fifties include this Saturday ritual. For rural children, going to see a picture show was just as exciting—and often a rare treat.

In comparative terms, we had few organized activities outside the home. Family activities were more the norm, a reality made possible by large families and, most often, the presence of extended family in the community.

Teens created their own amusements, dancing, making music, playing games and dating. They listened to records and music on the radio, music that came over the border from the United States. Popular music was innocuous, performed by singers who were just as innocuous in dress and manner. Late at night the radio signal from the United States was clear, bringing music and commercials from as far away as Oklahoma. This music was western, epitomized by the steel guitar and nasal twang of the Nashville singers; spirituals played during evangelical broadcasts; the ballads of crooners; the swing music of big bands. The commercials mirrored the American way of life.

Then came television. The first television sets displayed snowy images but the medium fascinated the children of the fifties as it brought the world into our living rooms. We watched and were shaped by American sitcoms, westerns and the world of Disney. Davy Crockett and his coonskin hat were as popular with young children in western Canada as anywhere in the United States. Anything the fledgling television industry in Canada produced rated a poor second in our eyes.

Teenagers (a term first coined in 1948) readily adopted the fads and fancies portrayed on television and just as eagerly embraced the music that wafted from the US on their newly invented portable, battery-operated radios. Radio stations quickly switched to music formats, leaving drama to the visual medium of television. And the music the stations played was just as new and untried as the new radio formats. The music was rock 'n' roll.

Ask children of the fifties who lived in western Canada what being a teenager of the time meant to us and we will invariably say, "Elvis Presley." A Cleveland disc jockey first used the term "rock 'n' roll" to describe the music that Elvis and his contemporaries performed. Parents found it objectionable stuff—laden with suggestive lyrics, a raw beat—and raucous movement—all displayed in their living rooms when television finally brought us Elvis in 1956. When he dressed in pink and black, teenagers throughout western Canada sported pink and black outfits. When he styled his hair in a sweeping "ducktail," teenage boys throughout the Canadian west followed suit, as did some girls.

Keeping abreast of the new groups and releases was easier now that television presented the world. As well, technology had produced the LP, a twelve-inch, long-playing vinyl record, and the seven-inch single, unbreakable 45 rpm (revolutions per minute) record that sold for under a dollar and played on phonographs that cost as little as $12.95. Very few of the performers favoured by teenagers in the fifties were Canadians.

By the end of the 1950s, television and rock 'n' roll music were a regular and accepted part of the lives of fifties young people. Some could not remember a time when television and rock 'n' roll did not exist.

▷ **Peter P., born in 1935**
grew up on a farm near Winlaw in southern British Columbia

There used to be some dances, locally held, and there was a store where people gathered every evening to play cards or tell jokes or dance to record music. They had a record player. My brother had a gramophone that you had to crank up.

The store was just a small one where you got cigarettes and chocolate bars and things like that. There was a stove in there. The store was run by a person who was disabled. He had had a logging accident and got slammed against a tree or something. There used to be a gas pump too, where you pumped the gas by hand.

I'm of the Doukhobor religion so we don't believe in church but we do have meetings. I used to belong to this young persons' group, up to thirty years old, you could belong. We had drama groups, discussions, things like that. More or less trying to keep up our own culture. We still do have the festivals every year. All winter we would be getting ready for that. Adults would actually participate too. They'd get something prepared, maybe a discussion about something or other. They pretty well kept the younger people in line. Most of the time though, they would just keep out of it and give encouragement. Then, the high school kids had a tough time participating because they had homework to do. We didn't have homework so it was okay for us.

We didn't have that much money but it wasn't so tough. We didn't have technology like TVs, VCRs and other high-powered machines. If somebody had a car, well, he was lucky. We listened to the radio. Old-time music from Calgary and comedy shows like "Dagwood." We had a Marconi radio that sat on the table and a floor model but it didn't work so well.

We lived a mile from the store and every Sunday the woman at the store would get a big can of ice cream. There was no freezers at that time so the ice cream was packed in insulation so it wouldn't melt. But you hurried over there in the morning because by noon it would be all gone. I think it was five cents a cone. I ate so much of it then that I don't like it any more.

A package of tobacco at that time used to cost twenty cents and five cents for papers and then penny matches, so twenty-five cents would get you all this. A package of cigarettes was thirty-five cents. It was cheaper to buy the tobacco and make your own. There was Ogdens and Players. But Ogdens was the most popular one. I don't know if there is any Ogdens any more. I quit smoking about twenty-five years ago so I don't even know what brands they have. I think there was an Old Chum brand.

▷ **Jim, born in 1937**
 grew up in Pipestone, Manitoba

We used to go to the Brandon Fair once every year or two. That was a big event. It took all day to get in there. We had an old Buick, one of those old square ones.

What did I do for fun? Well, once I remember I painted my brother with a spray gun. We were painting the barn and he came around the corner and I had a hold of the gun and I painted him red right from one end to the other. I got it with the crib board that time—fifteen-two, fifteen-four and a pair is six. It was worth it. He looked great red.

When I was a teenager, I travelled all over the country going to dances. I played trumpet in a combo orchestra—that was before rock 'n' roll. Furthest we'd go was seventy-five or a hundred miles. We didn't make a great deal of money. Me and my cousin, a piano player, and a saxophone player and a drummer. Max White's Band. Max White was the man who played the sax.

▷ **Elaine, born in 1938**
grew up in the village of Botha, Alberta

When you tried to smoke, it was a really bad sin. I can remember going for a walk with some of the kids and some of them were pretty cool. They'd swear at the drop of a hat. We walked for probably a mile and a half and me trying to work into a sentence how I could very casually say "damn" and be cool.

We went to dances. I loved to dance. We always went to church and I belonged to CGIT (Canadian Girls in Training) and had a lot of fun with that. I always went to summer camp—even when my mother forced me to go when I was older. But I had the best time I ever had in my life.

Both sides of the family were musical. My friends and I would come home from school and one of my friends played the guitar and we would just play the piano and sing. That was our big entertainment. In about 1954 or '55, Grandpa and Grandma got a TV. There was only about two TVs in town. So every Sunday night Grandpa and Grandma's house was absolutely packed with kids.

▷ **Gary, born in 1938 in Manitoba**
grew up in Vancouver, British Columbia

Our first stereo set was a Motorola. It looked like a suitcase that you take apart and just spread the speakers out. A home stereo unit.

At this time in Vancouver, CBC was the only television station. We had a television set called a Sylvania Halolight and it had a light around the screen. Then we got a Rogers Majestic. I always liked to watch wrestling. And Bob Fortune, he was the weatherman. Everybody liked to watch him. Back in those days, we were even impressed with the test pattern when television first came out. We got TV about 1954 and we watched Jackie Gleason, Art Carney and "The Honeymooners." I loved them. Ed Sullivan was on. "I've Got A Secret"—I believe Gary Moore was the host of that. And we watched "Truth or Consequences."

When I was in high school, it was every boy's dream to have a motorized bike. There was a bike called a Whizzer. It was like a CCM balloon-tire bicycle that you pedalled, and it had a big belt on this little 98cc or 49cc engine that would get the thing going. There was another bike, which actually looked like a girl's bike, from England called a Francis. It was a little 98cc bike that you'd get going and then it would take over by itself. Like mopeds today. I remember sitting on my Tri-

Gary and Rita on his motorcycle, circa 1951.

umph Tiger 100 motorcycle and going down to Kerrisdale Arena, trying to pick up girls.

It was always a highlight in my life going to the BC Lions football games. And being there the first time they ever beat the Edmonton Eskimos. I was there in the famous fog bowl. I saw Billy Graham in Empire Stadium one Sunday afternoon with my mother. We sat way up on top. I saw the 1956 Grey Cup Game in Vancouver. After the Grey Cup, they had the Shriner's All-Star Game. I went to that Shriner's Game and after that the plane carrying the football players crashed into the mountain near Chilliwack.

I went to the British Empire Games and saw John Landy and Roger Bannister running the Miracle Mile. Hosting the Empire Games in Vancouver was really something for the city. The publicity built up between John Landy and Roger Bannister for the Miracle Mile made it the sports event of the time. It was all we heard about on the radio. So I went.

When I was going to Lord Byng High School in Vancouver the fad was a boogie cut; it was a brush cut on the top with the hair on the sides combed back with lots of Brylcreem and a ducktail in the back. Brushcuts were kind of in but the boogie cut was big. The Elvis type of cut was really in too, with all your hair combed back in a ducktail.

We would buy dress pants with a real nice taper so you could hardly get your foot in them. And guys would want to have their comb sticking out of their back pocket. Black leather jacket and sometimes a pink shirt. Like Jimmy Dean, you would wear your collar up with your ducktail. The girls would wear long skirts down to their ankles and they'd have a small purse with a long strap that they'd kind of drag along the floor. Everyone chewed gum and the Hula Hoop was popular. I remember Buddy Holly and the Crickets were big, Elvis, Chuck Berry, Fats Domino, the Diamonds.

We went to the pool hall a lot. No girls allowed there. I liked a lot of girls but I was too bashful to take many out. The first girl I took out was a Sunday School teacher who had moved over from Scotland. Her name was Rita. I took her skating on Lost Lagoon in Stanley Park in Vancouver. I borrowed my dad's 1956 Plymouth—that was my dad's first car in maybe twenty years.

One of the interesting things about the fifties was, well, I smoked, everyone smoked, and I took a drink. The fifties were pre-drugs so we would drink. I remember three of us guys going away on a long weekend up to a lake near Hope. We'd go up there and take a mickey and we'd get high and think that we were really going all out. Sixteen. Fishing and thinking, Wow, we've maybe got too much liquor with us!

I played drums in a band. A little group with drums, piano and guitar. We thought we were pretty good. We took a record that we had made to Jack Cullen, host of the "Night Owl Show" on CKNW. He said, "You guys got potential."

▷ **Dwayne, born in 1939**
   grew up in Brandon, Manitoba

I had my own personal radio, a little Motorola. In about 1948, Dad brought it across the border and I had it all the time I was growing up. During the daytime you listened to CKX because you really couldn't get too much else, but in the evening, after the sun went down, you could pick up stations from quite a distance away, sometimes as far off as WLS in Chicago.

I travelled enough to know that I liked home as well as any place on earth. We travelled in the States and Canada. Usually it was in the winter. We would go down to Phoenix or California, and spend some time. There was another trip to Chicago and St. Louis in the summertime. That would have been 1949. We went to a professional baseball game on that trip. It was boiling hot in St. Louis and the humidity was even higher than the temperature was. We couldn't get home fast enough. Dad travelled either for farm machinery business or because he was the lieutenant governor of the Kiwanis Club, both of which meant he did a fair bit of travelling. He also travelled with the barbershop singers. Both of us, well, not me until later, but in those days he was a barber-shopper. We would do a bit of travelling around with them.

I had a different childhood than a lot of the kids around because most of them didn't travel like that. I always considered myself fairly worldly. I knew most of the western states in those days. Later on in life, I covered all of the United States and eventually Europe.

All the boys around our area had a nickname—mine was "Pike." Don't ask why. It just happened.

A lot of the boys, when they were, say, thirteen and up, would join Army or Air Cadets. In my case it was the Army Cadets. I really enjoyed it. It was something that I think a lot of kids now miss out on. It taught you to be a little disciplined, to look after yourself, to take your hat off when you go into a room, good manners. I was sitting at supper tonight watching two or three adults, or so-called adults, sitting there eating their supper with their baseball caps on in a restaurant. I was all for going up and telling them off. If I was their lieutenant at that time I'd have been screaming at them. I know that's a very minor thing but the Cadets would have straightened them out.

I remember when the Green Acres Drive-In Theatre opened in north Brandon. It was a Famous Players Theatre. That would have been way back, 1949 or '50, somewhere in there. The first drive-in I ever went to was in Minot, but it was shortly after that, probably that same summer, that they built this one in Brandon.

The first drive-in restaurant was called "The Train." It was an old streetcar. In 1910 or 1911 streetcars came to Brandon but the system only lasted a year and a half. Five streetcars were put on a lot at the end of town and left there. They were new when they were put there and they stayed there until 1950 or so. They took three of the cars and put them end-to-end on a lot at 27th and Victoria. One was used for storage, another was used for cooking and the third one was where you went to get your order. They'd pass it out to you or sometimes they'd have people there serving you in the car. Carhops didn't really come here until A&W arrived.

▷ Marilyn, born in 1940
grew up at Lake Cowichan, British Columbia

One of the things I remember as a teenager, going down to a dance at Ladysmith when Red Robinson was deejay. We danced to records, 78s. We danced up a storm. Of course it was at the very beginning of the rock 'n' roll era.

I was a cheerleader in a long pleated skirt. This was about '54 or '55. I'm sure we were the only cheerleaders in the world who didn't have short skirts. We had long white pleated skirts that came below our knees. I don't know why they were so long, maybe it was more ladylike.

We used to have sock hops in the high school gymnasium. We had a lot of inter-school basketball and volleyball games, mostly basketball. Friday nights were the big basketball night. We would go, with our long skirts, as cheerleaders to a school somewhere else on Vancouver Island or our own gym if a team was visiting. That was Friday night entertainment.

I remember not having a television set in the house and going to a friend's on Sunday night to watch Ed Sullivan when Elvis was the guest star.

▷ **Audrey H., born in 1941**
grew up on a farm near Strongfield in south-central Saskatchewan

There seemed to be lots of rain in the 1950s and one of our pastimes was rafting on sloughs. One of my brothers built a raft and we carried it quite a distance to a slough in our neighbour's pasture.

In the fifties, we were community people. No one travelled much, so movies were a big part of our entertainment. The local community hall had movies Wednesday and Saturday nights, and I remember lots of musicals, like *Annie Get Your Gun* and *Showboat*. Our parents were selective in the movies we saw, but they missed on one—*The Thing*. It caused me many a nightmare and to this day I remember the gory parts.

Two radio programs that we could not miss were "Maggie Muggins" and "Just Mary." "Just Mary" was on Sunday mornings and "Maggie Muggins" was on about 4:30 on a weekday.

Dances were held in the hall on Friday and Saturday nights. During the late fifties they were building the Gardiner Dam and workers would be at the dances. Quite often a fist fight would occur. At every dance the orchestra would stop playing for a half-hour at midnight and everyone had lunch. There would be no liquor in the hall in those days but most people had a drink or two in a vehicle outside.

In our small village, as in most small villages, we had a Chinese restaurant. It was a hangout for teenagers. For us, a trip to a larger town was a big event. It was an even bigger deal to have dinner or even just ice cream in the Chinese cafe. There was a drugstore in our neighbouring town and a part of the store was a soda shop. There were small round tables and chairs with a fancy scrolled back. There we would have an ice cream soda—that was so good! Just the smell was delicious.

In the summertime, each district in the area had an annual picnic. Ours was held at the country school. There were races and games for the children, plus a final ball game that included everyone who could swing a bat. There was a lot of visiting as one didn't see neighbours too often. The biggest event of the day was when the store owner from town brought the ice cream. It was transported in canvas containers with ice packed in around the ice cream cartons. What a treat.

I remember Saskatchewan's fiftieth anniversary celebration in 1955. There were floats and parades and a big community get-together. It was a big thing for a farm kid—parades especially.

Mom was an excellent seamstress so she made a lot of our clothes. For Christmas she would look in the catalogue for a style, order the material from either Eaton's or Simpson's and, without a pattern, sew up a dress. When flared skirts with crinolines were popular she sewed the skirts and we bought one or two crinolines, to be in style. When strides, flared-leg slacks tapered to a narrow bottom, were the fad, she made our neighbour girl and I a pair each. They were charcoal with pink—very popular colours at that time.

We'd go to Saskatoon maybe once a year and I remember going to Woolworth's to buy lipstick. When my mom said I could buy lipstick, I think I was in grade nine. We saved what we could of our allowance, so we had maybe $5 for those trips to Saskatoon.

The ducktail hairstyle was very popular in the fifties and both boys and girls had them. The hair was held in place by a thick gel, Dippity Doo, all combed to meet at the back of the head in a ducktail. We usually didn't have to comb our hair during the day at all!

The style leaders in the fifties wore cardigan sweater sets and would often wear just the cardigan, buttoned down the back. Saddle shoes and bobby socks were a must. In the later part of the fifties, pleated plaid skirts were very popular and we would wear leotards with them in the winter.

If you were dating someone you'd wear his ring with yards of tape so it would fit. I think the guys wore the girl's ring on a chain around their neck—at least one of mine did.

▷ **Steve, born in 1941 in Edmonton**
moved to Williams Lake, British Columbia, in 1953

For toys we had some magnificent German wind-up cars. They were pretty neat and sturdy, and then there was the cheap Japanese stuff made of tin. And we had box cameras. We played shinny in Edmonton. Using shovels, we pried the compacted snow off the sidewalks, stood it up and tramped it down to make a rink. It wasn't ice but the next best thing. It was cold in the wintertime in Alberta, everyone got their tongues stuck on something metal at one point or another. I read Classic Comics and was a pretty good trader. I didn't have the massive comic collection that some did though. I believed they were for reading, not hoarding.

After we moved to Williams Lake, we had horses. The PGE railroad sold a bunch of lots above the town and we built a house there. With nothing but ranch land in behind, the horses could range free all the time. We kept a garbage can full of oats on the back porch. We'd rattle the garbage can and they'd come thundering down to eat.

I had a wonderful group of guys who were my friends. One of them had the highest IQ in the whole school and was seen as kind of a nerd. He's our accountant now.

I got my driver's licence four hours after I turned sixteen. As a teenager, I didn't drink and I still don't. Some of my friends were in a Volkswagen and were drinking and got into an accident. They all died. My father was the doctor who did the post-mortems. He took me with him to see it. It was a strong lesson.

My friends and I used to go downtown and park our cars and watch the fights. The cowboys would fight each other but they never bothered us. They were more likely to give you a beer or offer you a mickey of gin.

▷ **Maxine, born in 1942**
grew up in Gypsumville, Manitoba

We didn't get television until 1960, after I left home. But we listened to the radio—"Boston Blackie," "I was a Communist for the FBI," "Our Miss Brooks," "Ford Theatre." On Saturday morning there was Porky Charbonneau and his "Top Twenty." He would count down the songs from twenty, then nineteen, eighteen and so on. The radio ran on a car battery. It was on a little stand in the living room with all the acid leaking out all over. When it was forty below and the car wouldn't start in the morning, you'd take the battery from the radio, put it in the car and start the car.

We spent a fair bit of time reading because my mother had been a teacher. We had a whole wall full of books. We played Monopoly by the hour. When I was about eleven, I learned to play bridge—it was actually a plot to keep my brother off the street. He was fourteen and what was there for him to do? So we played bridge—my dad and I against my mom and my brother. We played bridge by the hour in the wintertime.

We didn't have very much in the way of fashion because all of our clothes came from the Sears' or Eaton's catalogues. Although, my mother had come from Dominion City, so she knew about cities and things. She would write letters to the Hudson's Bay shopper describing what she would like for us. They would send it and sometimes it was suitable and sometimes it wasn't, but it meant that we sometimes had stuff that wasn't in the catalogue. We did have saddle shoes, white bucks and then we got pink bucks. That was just the height of fashion! We had felt skirts with poodles and other things on them. We used Jo-Cur setting gel. We couldn't always get it so Mother used to concoct something from flaxseed—you could boil flaxseed and make the same stuff.

▷ **Peter B., born in 1942 in England**
   came to Canada in 1944 and grew up in Regina, Saskatchewan

As kids growing up, my friends and I made our own fun—sometimes dangerous fun. In the winter we'd ride the bus bumpers—grab the bumper and drag behind on the icy roads. Then one day one of my friend's feet hit the concrete and his face hit the pavement. He scraped his face pretty bad. That ended our bumper riding. Because school was fifteen blocks away, we had often ridden the milk and bread truck bumpers in winter, too.

We lived near the railway yards and we'd sometimes ride the boxcars to the movies on Dewdney Avenue—that's where the train slowed down and we'd jump off. Sometimes we'd lay between the tracks while the trains were shunting back and forth. We'd sit up on the signal lights and of course the trains needed those lights to know which track they were going on. Security guys pulled us off and told us we could go to jail for that prank.

▷ **Rupee, born in 1943 in India**
   came to Canada in 1947 and grew up in Victoria, British Columbia

As a teenager, being cool was if you dared to have a cigarette. If you were really, really daring you'd have a gulp of beer without your mom and dad finding out about it. The other cool thing was wearing long, sleeveless cardigan sweaters. That was a rage for a long time. When we were about fifteen or sixteen, we started wearing long trench-coat-style overcoats. They were reversible. When I bought my first one, I paid $12 for it.

Because we were East Indian, we were not allowed to date. If we wanted to go to a dance, my parents would drive us there and pick us up. We weren't allowed to walk with a group to the dance, because we didn't want to be with the "bad element." My dad kept very, very close, stringent tabs on us because his belief was, if you grew up in this culture, you could take advantage of all the things that were offered but, as an East Indian, the proper thing to do was to go back to India and get married. I didn't do that. I think I let my father down drastically. I had my first date during my first year in university—that's when I first had the nerve to ask a girl out.

▷ **Bob, born in 1943**
grew up in Regina, Saskatchewan

I grew up on Victoria Avenue, in the west end. I remember going out and playing hide-and-go-seek in the spring and the fall when it was starting to get dark early. At that time there were ditches on both sides of Victoria Avenue and old wooden sidewalks. At the intersections the street was dug out underneath. I used to crawl up and hide underneath the wooden sidewalks. The other kids would be running back and forth on the sidewalks and I would be hiding underneath. They were great hiding places back then.

Another thing I remember about Victoria Avenue was that we had a big old house and right across the street, across Victoria Avenue, there was a huge market garden. It was called the relief gardens. They were started in the thirties and people could get little plots of land and grow some carrots and onions or whatever. Those gardens were there the whole time I was growing up. We did the usual kid things. The relief gardens got raided and we'd take a couple of carrots. No big thing.

Right beside the gardens to the north was the CPR mainline. All the freight and passenger trains ran up and down that track at all hours of the day and night. Adjacent to that were the provincial exhibition grounds. Our house had a big full verandah on it and my brothers and I had the bedroom upstairs at the front of the house. We would climb out on the roof of the verandah and watch the exhibition. You could watch everything going on.

While the exhibition was on, Victoria Avenue would be packed with cars at night because people would come and park all along the avenue and sit in their cars and watch the fireworks. But we sat on the roof of the verandah and watched. It was great!

At about age eleven or twelve, somewhere in there, I started getting to go to drive-in movies because my sister, the one next to me in
age, was dating and it always made Dad feel better if I was along. Of
course it didn't do a helluva lot of good because we'd get to the drive-
in and I'd be fast asleep in the back seat. But Dad always felt better
about it.

Summers were good times. I got to stay up later and we would go
up to Waskesui every summer. The first time we went was probably
about 1949 or 1950, somewhere in there. Dad bought a cabin there, I
think the grand price was about $100. We had that place until the
sixties and we spent a lot of good times up there.

▷ **John, born in 1943**
grew up in Winnipeg, Manitoba

We really identified with the West. It would have been an insult to say
we were easterners. I was an avid Winnipeg Blue Bomber fan and would
hope they'd beat the Edmonton Eskimos, but it was crucially important that they beat the Hamilton Tiger Cats or whoever it was from
back east. Our heroes were the guys on the Winnipeg Blue Bombers.

In winter we used to play street hockey or we'd go to the ice rink—
an open, outdoor ice rink. In the summer we used to play football on the
street. Sometimes we'd go down to the Red River which wasn't far away.

I had an uncle who had a television. He was the rebel in his family.
When it started out, there used to be a lot of westerns on so we used to
go over there and watch endless horse opera. To this day I can't stand
horse opera unless it's really unusual. I remember seeing a pamphlet
that the church put out which was against television. It's ironic today
that we don't have a television and my mother does. In the same vein,
at one point we weren't allowed to read comics. I'm not sure why. The
ironic thing in that is I ended up drawing comics for a Mennonite
magazine.

We weren't allowed to go to theatres. The only time we went to a
theatre was to see the Coronation. The pastor of our church went to
the school to discuss this. I guess he gave them permission to take the
kids to the theatre for the Coronation. I think we managed to see part
of a war movie too. That was really exciting for us. The first movie I
saw was *Ben Hur* and I think my parents didn't think it was very good
that I had gone to do that. Not based on *Ben Hur*, but just the idea of
going to a theatre.

We didn't go downtown much. On Saturday nights, my dad used to take us for a ride. We always wanted to head into town and he wanted to head out of town. We usually ended up going out of town and he'd buy us ice cream or something.

My brother and I didn't get along very well and we used to fight. I used to hang around with three or four guys. As we got older, we got into electronics and model airplanes. The most memorable Christmas gift I ever had was an electric train. I thought that was the ultimate toy. It must have cost my dad a bit of money.

I loved radio and I used to listen to the radio drama shows. The radio had those glowing tubes and it might not even have had a case around it. I would lie in bed at night and see if I could get far away stations. We used to be able to pick up KXEL in Waterloo, Iowa. They would have offers that would end at midnight tomorrow night. I re-member that. "Ten-ninety-five until midnight tomorrow night," the announcer would say.

When I was a little shaver, I took violin lessons and I did quite well until the teacher decided he was going back to university. I had to go somewhere else and I didn't like that, so that was the end of music lessons. And at some point I got a guitar and started learning that. I enjoyed that. We had a piano in the house. The girls took piano lessons but the boys didn't. They offered me violin.

As a kid I was fascinated by trains. In Winnipeg you could go down-town to the CPR station and go down underneath the tracks and you'd hear the trains rumbling above you. Things really have changed—then the idea of trains was fascinating but the idea of planes were beyond us altogether. They were for people who could afford it. Now my moth-er's the one who flies.

On Sunday when we came home from church I used to listen to a Portage La Prairie radio station that used to have kind of Christian country music. People like the Chuckwagon Gang. If I heard that stuff now I think I'd turn it off—fast! But in those days, I liked it. But my parents didn't appreciate that.

A number of the Mennonites had a cultured view of music. They had a Mennonite orchestra and were into classical music. But my par-ents weren't into that.

Like every other kid, I liked Elvis and the Beatles. My brother brought home an album of Elvis singing hymns. My father said, "That's like eating a meal out of a slop pail."

▷ **Lil, born in 1944**
grew up in and near Nampa in northern Alberta

I enjoyed the farm. I could take my red plastic guitar and go over to the stoneboat and sit and sing to my heart's content. My singing was pretty bad so the rest of the family encouraged me to sing as far away from the house as I could.

I loved lying in the wonderful fields of clover, surrounded by wonderful smells, making the clouds into anything I wanted them to be. I spent hour upon hour daydreaming and it was fabulous. Oh, to be able to be a child again. On the other hand, what's stopping me from doing that now?

Uncle Mike and Aunt Ann didn't live that far away so we had the opportunity to rabbit hunt with my cousins, Victor and Eddie. One evening we wounded a rabbit and it made a sound very much like a newborn baby. My dad sent us back out to track it because we couldn't leave it like that. After hours of searching we still couldn't find it. I have never forgotten that sound.

A parking lot was our playground for afternoons of scrub ball. It seemed that I'd spend hours in the field chasing the ball, then only seconds up to bat before they would strike me out and back to the field I'd go. One time I refused to get off the batter's base. The next batter up tried to get me to move but I refused, holding up the game, so he swung the bat and got me in the head. That resulted in a trip to the hospital in Peace River and my first haircut.

One year for holidays we went to Tacoma, Washington, to visit Dad's relatives. The ocean was beyond belief! The city was massive and so was their home. They had a TV which I promptly attached myself to. I was watching a show about an escaped convict who entered a farm home and had a knife to the lady's throat, when the TV went blank. I sat there staring at that blank screen for hours, waiting for it to come back on. When it finally did, it was an entirely different show. I was shocked that the show I was watching did not reappear and that the ending was lost forever. My fascination with the TV ended abruptly.

As a teenager, I was always busy going to CGIT meetings and camp, pajama parties, bike riding, skating on the backwaters at the river, basketball and carving my initials in trees with those of my special person—Ricky Nelson. I remember blue jeans, baggy sweaters, ball games and card parties at home. My favourite shows were anything to do with Debbie Reynolds such as *Tammy and the Bachelor* and *Tammy Goes to Paris.*

I remember going on a trip to Saskatchewan to visit Mom's relatives. The three of us girls were scrunched in the back seat of the car and, of course, we all had our hair in ringlets and had dresses with crinolines. Oh, were they scratchy! We starched those crinolines with sugar and water and if we went to a special dance, we wore three of them at once.

I spent my money on essentials, such as penny loafers, bobby socks, pom-pom skirts and can-cans in different colours. I slowly got over Ricky Nelson and the love of my life became Elvis. The boys at school were getting interesting. During grade nine I got permission to date in groups one evening per week, but still had to be home by ten. This broadened my horizons. We now went to hockey games in nearby towns. My parents insisted on making me wear those ugly green wool ski pants. No problem. I'd go to Sheila's, take them off, borrow her jeans and switch again before returning home.

We learned the jive flip with only a few minor accidents to walls and nearby spectators. Groups of us went bowling for the first time in Peace River. Everywhere we went the vehicle would be packed like a sardine can. I wanted to go everywhere with my older sisters so one evening when I was refused permission to go out, I snuck out the bedroom window with them and went to the dance at the community hall. Upon returning we crawled back through the window and into bed only to find Dad in our room waiting for us. Needless to say, I was still grounded until the 1960s rolled around.

▷ **Linda H., born in 1944**
grew up on a farm near Marsden, Saskatchewan

We wore slacks and full skirts and penny loafers. And crinolines for dress-up school dances. I loved to spend an hour or so starching that thing and ironing it. It was so classy. At the dances we did a lot of square dances. Orchestras all the time except for school dances. We always had a record hop. You'd have a little carrying case for 45s and sometimes you'd trade with your friends. I remember pin curls and I wore a pony tail. My hair is naturally curly and fluffy but I did perm it anyway at one point. That was the worst disaster of my whole life.

We didn't have TV. People down the road had it and an aunt and uncle had it. We used to all rush over there and peer at the snow. As children, we thought it was great but our parents thought this was pretty silly. I listened to the radio. I loved Burl Ives. He had a folk music half-hour every Saturday afternoon.

▷ **JoAnne, born in 1944**
grew up in Dawson City, Yukon

In 1949 my father tore down a vacant building he owned in town. With the material from that, he built a cabin at Rock Creek. Rock Creek was only a few miles from town but it became a place for people to go on weekends and for summer holidays. We all loved it there and always felt as if we had been away on a great holiday whenever we spent time at the cabin. Sometimes in the summer, my father would drive the family out to the cabin. We would stay there while he commuted back and forth to town. He could take care of the store while we were at the cabin.

We very seldom took trips. Other than going to the cabin, we did make a couple of short trips into Alaska. Once, my mother took the three kids to Vancouver. We went to see our grandparents. She was combining this visit with a buying trip for merchandise for the store. I was only six at the time but I can remember just about every detail of that summer. We went to Whitehorse in a small plane and then got in a bigger plane. Vancouver was such a thrill. We could not have imagined in our wildest dreams what a big city would be like. We went to Stanley Park, to the five and dime store, to the circus and to the beach. We saw fruit trees for the first time. We took a ferry to Bowen Island to see our grandpa. We saw a farm. When we left Vancouver to go back home, we took a cruise ship up the Inside Passage. When we reached Skagway, we got on the train to go to Whitehorse. The entire trip was a series of new adventures, things I have never forgotten.

In Dawson City, we lived downtown and there was only one other girl my age, the rest were boys. I was kind of a tomboy and my friends and I spent a lot of time building forts. We scrounged wood from old buildings and from the garage. Some of these forts became our little schoolhouse or our clubhouse and sometimes there would be small neighbourhood turf wars going on. Our little buildings were moved up and down the alley, depending on how relationships were going. These disputes never lasted very long and things would go back to normal. We built little boats we could sail in the pond and the swamp. We built rafts and played on them in the swamp. We had a lot of fun building what we called go-carts—they were made out of egg crates. We'd go to the dump and get wheels off old bicycles. We had a lot of fun doing that. When Dawson City hit its low ebb, a lot of businesses closed—restaurants, hotels and stores. And when the people left, they left everything here. If we wanted to play restaurant, we went to a vacant restaurant. All the dishes were still there. And if we wanted to play hotel, we just went to a vacant hotel. The beds were still there. The furniture was still there. I don't ever remember being bored. There was always something to do. We made our own fun. There were lots of times we didn't have a movie theatre, didn't have much else to go to. We didn't get TV in Dawson City until the sixties.

We used to sit around the radio as a family and listen to stories they'd play. Sometimes my younger brother and I would sit on Dad's knee and he'd read us comics. He liked to read to us. My dad loved music so we had a record player and played a lot of records all the time. Music of the forties and fifties.

We had wonderful Christmases. The people of Dawson put on wonderful Christmas galas that included plays or skits from each school class. Everyone in town would be there. After grades one to twelve put on their skits, we then had a visit from Santa Claus. He gave out a small bag of candy to each and every child who sat on his knee and told him what she or he wanted for Christmas. Following this, there was a dance for both adults and children. This was a time when fathers danced with daughters and sons danced with mothers. Everyone was dressed in their finest attire. It was great.

My family spent hours decorating the store windows for the holiday season. This was always a wonderful time. My father loved to play music and at Christmas he had it playing so it could be heard out on the street. On December 22 or 23 we always went out and cut down our Christmas tree, brought it home and decorated it. Decorating the tree and the house always resulted in much activity. I fondly remember the Christmas baking. My dad would put on a cook's hat and apron. Flour and sugar ended up all over the kitchen. The aroma of cheese straws, mince tarts, Christmas pudding and cookies filled the house. Then, of course, there was the polishing of the silver and making sure the crystal was sparkling.

When my parents had the store, they'd stay open late Christmas Eve. My mother and I would gift-wrap the presents, my two brothers would put them in a box on the toboggan and deliver them all over town. My father would escort some of his friends into the kitchen for a little liquid Christmas cheer.

But one year at Christmas time, my brother and I got chicken pox. And in those days if you had chicken pox you had to be quarantined. So my parents had to close the store. We couldn't have any family over for Christmas. So that was a strange one.

We were a year or two behind Vancouver in the music. It seemed to take that much longer to get here. We were always behind. But I remember the poodle skirts, the crinolines and always a little scarf around your neck. And pony tails. And the guys with low-riding jeans and jet boots, combs sticking out of their back pockets, trucker's wallets and leather jackets. And I remember I was a big Doris Day fan and I wanted my hair to look like Doris Day's. She had sort of short blond hair with a ducktail.

JoAnne as a teenager.

When I was about twelve, several girls got together and formed the Polly Pigtail Club. We had a clubhouse where we met frequently and we would look through the *Polly Pigtails Club Magazine*. This is where we decided to try smoking. One day one of us accidentally dropped a cigarette butt into a chair. We were so worried it was going to catch fire we poured countless buckets of water on the chair to make sure the butt was out. We did not want to smell of cigarette smoke so we all washed our mouths out with Ivory soap before we went home.

▷ **Denise, born in 1944**
  grew up in Regina, Saskatchewan

As I remember the fifties, everybody was light-hearted then. We did a lot of laughing. We used to go to drive-in theatres. I was one of the smallest so I was usually the one who hid in the trunk of the car—you know, to get in free. Beer was a big thing but because I didn't like beer I didn't get into that. I remember the beehive hairdos, although maybe that was more in the sixties. And I remember heavy make-up—it tended to hide the pimples.

▷ **Dennice, born in 1944**
  grew up on a farm near Dodsland, Saskatchewan

Going to town on Saturday was the highlight of the week. You'd clean the whole house, wash the car and curl your hair in pin curls and then hope that Dad would come in from whatever he was doing and get ready to go to town before it got too late. Late Saturday afternoon, you would polish the men's shoes on the doorstep to go to town. You'd have to scrape them first because in the part of Saskatchewan where I grew up the soil was gumbo and there was always mud on the shoes. You'd wash them off, wait for them to dry and then put the shoe polish on. At that time of day you could hear a tractor putt-putting home off in the distance, particularly our neighbour to the west because he had a John Deere. It was kind of the last thing you did—got the shoes polished and shined and lined up on the step. And then you'd have the tub out because Dad would have to have a bath. The table was set and the potatoes peeled and everything ready to go. It'd be about eight o'clock when we left for town.

I can remember all the people out on the sidewalks greeting each other and doing their grocery shopping, and I remember, when I was younger, my grandmother taking eggs into the store to sell and also going into town and meeting other kids my age and playing hopscotch on the sidewalk. We would always go to the Chinese restaurant for ice cream.

The fowl supper was held in the fall after the harvest, in the country school, the town hall or the church basement. The women in the community would stuff the turkeys and cook them and bake pies and make gravy. At the country school, they would have to take it all made to the school because there was no kitchen facilities there. There would be long tables and benches set up—the same benches they would use for the dances and for church. On the tables were bowls of potatoes, dressing, cole slaw, vegetables, jellied salads, corn and pickles. Buns and butter and lots of pie. All homemade. And, of course, the turkey.

At the same time the women would cater most of the weddings in the community. They would also take pies and buns to the rink for bonspiels and skating events, make lunches for any showers, help with school picnics and for the sports days. You didn't need to know the person getting married very well, but as a woman in the community you went to her shower and you took a gift and lunch.

In 1953 my dad had a Ford one-ton truck. He had three hoops made that he bolted to the truck box and put a tarp over the hoops. Created a chuckwagon effect. He put a mattress on the truck-box floor and threw in a box of cooking utensils and we went to Waskesiu. I remember my mother taking out the wash basin and putting it on the end of the picnic table. That's where we washed our hands and we had another basin to wash the dishes in. We ate at the cook shack. I can remember the wonderful smell

Dennice and her family with their Ford truck made into a camper ready to head out to Waskesiu.

of the fire. We saved our money so we could go roller-skating at Waskesiu. That roller-skating rink was wonderful and was great fun. We went quite often to Waskesiu and I remember the music at the roller-skating rink was the same every year. They never changed it.

In 1956 I was twelve and in the 4H Club. Achievement Day was at the local school and the agricultural rep would come to judge the calves. As well as the judging of the calves, there was the showing of the calves and a record book competition. Other 4H activities were square dancing, public speaking and curling. After Achievement Day, the winners would take their calves to the big show in Kerrobert. We had Demonstration Days when you'd meet at different farms and the 4H Extension people from the university would be out. One year I was selected to represent our district at the Inter-provincial 4H Club Week in Saskatoon. I also attended a 4H camp at Wakaw one summer. I got a couple of public-speaking trophies through 4H, too.

Dennice and her brother and sister with their 4H calves ready to show, 1956.

I remember as a teenager, after washing my hair, trying to dry it by staying outside on a warm day before we went to town. And during school nights going to bed with a wet head or later on when the hair dryers came out, going to sleep with the hair dryer on. It would take a long time to dry because long hair was very much in fashion.

▷ **Giuliana (Julia), born in 1944 in Italy**
came to Canada in 1953 and grew up in Michel, British Columbia

We always had people over at the house. Church on Sunday. Christmas and other holidays were big family times and we'd be all together as a family. We'd have a lot of friends pop in after church for a glass of wine.

We had lots of fun. We played cards and Italian games. There was music

Julia in 1958.

and the accordion was always there. And everybody would dance and sing a lot. They harmonized really, really well.

▷ **Anita, born in 1946**
grew up in Vancouver, British Columbia

One summer highlight came in the form of a really, really old Chinese vegetable man who, once a week, would make the rounds of various neighbourhoods in his old wooden van. The truck was a dark blue colour and I vividly recall the tan-coloured tarpaulin which shut the back from inquisitive eyes, especially mine. I was probably the nosiest child on the block, and I dearly loved peering into the depths of his truck when the canvas was pulled aside for a grown-up customer. His treat for us kids, if we were behaving, would be a chip of ice that he'd hack off an enormous block with a truly evil-looking pick. That was the tastiest ice in the whole, wide world!

That rickety old man and his truck were second in popularity only to the ice cream man whose bell could attract children and hard-working adults alike. My hard-earned nickel would nearly melt in my small, sweaty hand as I waited, impatiently, for the sight of his bicycle, the sound of the bell having caught my attention from several blocks away. Chocolate-covered ice cream bars were my favourite for ages, to be replaced by the more expensive "sandwiches" when I was much older. I still remember the delicious taste of them on humid summer days.

Sometimes I spent time in the Kootenay Valley at my grandparents' while my mother did relief nursing at the Kaslo Hospital. It was really different staying there. Gramps used to kill chickens to eat and I'll never forget the first time I saw one with its head chopped off. The chicken was running around while its head lay bleeding all over the chopping block. It was sad, but kind of funny at the same time.

I used to hide at the neighbour girl's house in her attic bedroom where she would show me pictures of Elvis Presley. My parents didn't like him at all. Of course, neither did hers, but she was four years older and got away with a lot more than I could.

My best friend from Vancouver used to visit us sometimes and, once, she and I hitchhiked. The guy who picked us up was probably twice our age (late twenties) and his car was a convertible. By the time he dropped us off a couple of blocks from my grandparents, we were terrified someone else would find out. No one ever did.

I managed to almost drown, once. It was at the Ainsworth pool, a hot springs north of Nelson on the way to Kaslo. I actually took three breaths, huge breaths, underwater before I somehow managed to get to the side of the pool. And the worst part of all was that my uncle wouldn't believe me when I said it was my cousin, *his daughter*, who had pushed me off the inner tube in the deep water. I slammed the screen door, I was so mad, and then I got a spanking. After nearly drowning! Boy, was that a bad day.

That same summer, I wanted to find out how mad bees got when a person poked a stick into the flower-planter base where their nest was. Talk about dumb. But I was just six years old.

In 1958, on Friday evenings, it was perfectly safe for twelve-year-old girls to take the bus downtown in Vancouver and go to a movie and catch the bus home again at about ten o'clock. However, going to a Saturday afternoon matinee was not safe by myself. I still can't remember the title of the show, but I do remember this creepy kind of man who sat beside me and kept putting his hand on my leg, just above my knee. I kept wiggling, trying to move further away. I was really afraid to yell out or even say a single word, except I started to cry. He said a really bad word, got out of his seat and disappeared into the dark. I wonder if he is still doing things like that to frighten little girls.

In those days, we could catch the dew worms on the boulevard across from Kitsilano Beach. At dusk, Dad and I used to dash around with flashlights to see where the biggest worms were sticking out of the ground. The best one I ever got was nearly nine inches long. A law against dew-worming was passed in the sixties because the area residents were bothered by the flashlights. Too bad. It was good, innocent fun.

When I was fifteen, my best friend and I tried to ski. I had my aunt's equipment from the 1930s and the very first day fell and broke my leg. A few years later I spent more time just helping to clear the cut beneath the Grouse Mountain chair lift, in early spring, than I did skiing. But I met some neat guys.

▷ **Ed, born in 1946**
  grew up in Saskatoon, Saskatchewan

I remember, in Saskatoon, the train station was downtown. We used to walk across this bridge which would span from what is now Idylwyld over to Second Avenue. I used to have to walk across that virtually every day because my high school was downtown.

My parents gave me what seems to me now inordinate freedom. I would wander. I was the kind of kid who would always get up early and I might leave at seven o'clock in the morning and come back at seven at night. I'd wander around the back alleys and I'd look at everything and—I just kind of wandered around a lot. There was no real worry at all. Same thing at the farm. From the time I was eight years old, I'd just take my gun and the dog and we'd go for the day. Just wander around shooting anything that moved, some things that didn't.

I remember finding stolen property and getting a reward. I was wandering in the park and found a briefcase—now I realize it was a travelling salesman's sample case. I had a good friend across the street, one year older than me. He and I got the reward. We chummed around together. We made explosives together.

I remember breaking into an abandoned auto wrecker's business. We needed parts. I remember dismantling a furnace and taking it out. All the electrical parts, the motor and transformer and that sort of stuff. Took it all out and never got caught.

I remember making explosives and electronic guns. We would make our own black powder by going to the library and figuring out the formula, then I would go and buy saltpeter. I'd have to go to different drugstores all over town and kind of wink when I bought it. Then I had to make charcoal by burning wood in the absence of air. We would take a piece of hardwood, put it in a tobacco can and, when our parents left, put it in the furnace. And when they came home the house was about 130 above in the middle of summer. We never did master the formula. If you had too much saltpeter it glowed and burned with an absolute white flame. I remember my father bought a new half-ton truck. He was quite proud of it. We put four or five tablespoons of the stuff on the bed of the truck and lit it. It took forever to light but when it did, it burned with a white, hot flame and it actually fell right through the truck. Melted right through the bed of the truck.

We made electric guns to keep the neighbourhood bullies in line. We were always geeks but they left us alone because we had the power to kill them. We could make what would now be called pipe bombs. We would make electric guns or take blocks of oak and drill holes in them, get a Model T Ford coil, hook it up to two nails at the bottom and pack it full of gunpowder, nails and a bunch of glass, stand hundred feet away, push the button and blow glass and rocks in front of them. It kept them away from us. They thought we were weird and kind of different. We had no intention to hurt them—we were too cowardly to do that—but they didn't know that.

When much of the lead pipes in houses was being switched to steel, we'd go down the back alleys and collect as much lead as we could. We'd melt it over a fire in the backyard, and then we'd pour it into the tops of bricks and make ingots. But they took too long to cool so we had a pot full of liquid lead and decided to pour water on it to cool it. Of course, it exploded. My friend didn't have a shirt on. I remember the whole front of his chest was plastered with pockmarks of melted lead. He's dead now. Died at thirty-five.

I remember radio before TV, and actually still enjoy radio more than TV. We'd lie on the floor in front of the radio and listen to programs like "The Lone Ranger."

I remember the name of the first record I ever bought in college, "Telstar" by the Tornadoes. I remember driving around a corner and the record slid out of the jacket and slid across the street. It didn't break the record, but it did make for a helluva scratchy record on one side!

▷ **Gail, born in 1946**
grew up in Prince Rupert, British Columbia

We wore reversible plaid skirts. They were sewn down on the hips and showed a different plaid when you wore it reversed. And I remember the little furry pom-poms on a velvet rope that you tied around your neck. Hair rollers—I spent a lot of time in rollers. And nylons. That was one of the big parts of growing up. I remember those garter belts. And a girdle, you had to have one of them. Our Home Economics teacher told us, "Girls, as soon as you have anything that wiggles, that's the time to get one of those little girdles." We were about fourteen then. She also told us that the back of the knee was the ugliest part of the female anatomy. That, of course, determined your skirt length.

▷ **Sandy, born in 1946**
grew up in Winnipeg, Manitoba

In the summer there would be excursions to visit my father's family at Gladstone—his mother and his brothers and sisters. My mother's family were a lot further away. They were in the Brandon area. When I was about twelve, I went to meet them all and there was quite a number of them spread out through the little towns. I remember one night my father driving off the muddy road in the snow in the country and having to get the tractor to pull us out. I thought that was really exciting.

Doing anything together was an incredible struggle for my family. The only thing we usually did was going to see my relatives on the farm. And it was more of going somewhere and being in someone else's space. The idea of us being together at all was usually uncomfortable and painful, so it was something to be avoided other than at the dinner table. My dad wasn't really into being a family person. He was quite a character. Wherever we went, he would be creating a scene or a ruckus. He was always interested in things and teasing people and was a public sort of person—just not with his family. That wasn't really where he was at. He and my mother mostly argued. He and my brother didn't get along. It wasn't very pleasant.

My parents had old-time records they used to play. I don't know who was singing but I remember one called "Roly Poly" and "The Yellow Rose of Texas." I got a record player when I was about four. A little one that had red and yellow records. I was so thrilled. I used to hide away and turn on this record player and just dance and dance and dance. It was the best thing that ever happened.

I remember going shopping downtown with my mother at Woolworth's and having a strawberry milkshake at their counter. I thought that was heaven.

When I was twelve, I went to a hairdresser to get a perm even though my hair was wavy. They put your head in a thing like a rocket and there was these electric curlers in there. They had me all rigged up to these electric curlers and one of them was burning my ear and I never said anything. I went through all this pain and I thought, Well, if this is what you have to do, this is really uncomfortable. I hated it. Oh boy. Never did do it again.

I wore a ponytail. That was my favourite thing. And we wore girdles. I think I did real damage to myself, trying to squeeze it all in. I remember in the locker room in gym class always looking around. I think that's where I figured out to wear a girdle. I saw these girls I admired and they had such lovely figures and I thought, Oh, is that what they do?

I remember my brother combing his hair. It was at least a foot long in front. He'd grease it down and he'd get out this comb. It was a work of art. It would take ages each morning until he got this wave. He had a ducktail and his hair was perfect for it. It just curled a little bit. He was quite proud of that.

I had this skirt that was like a circle. I remember one that was made of felt. It had little things sewed on it. Bobby socks and penny loafers. And crinolines. I got sent home once from school for wearing too many crinolines. I thought that was real status. I remember scarves. Lightweight ones. We all had those.

We used to really eat up those teen magazines with Elvis Presley and the Everly Brothers. It was a whole new world opening up. Elvis Presley, and going to the movies and screaming. And jiving. I remember having all these girls over to my house and saying, "We're gonna jive," and we did. I remember that first dance party. It was a real turnabouter. We knew we were different then, we had jived.

▷ **Candace, born in 1946**
grew up in Edmonton, Alberta

The thing that stands out most in my mind when I was a kid was Saturdays at the Roxy Theatre on 124th Street. Every Saturday we'd get a quarter and we'd go to the theatre. It cost fifteen cents to get into the movies and you'd buy a horseshoe sucker and something else. That's what I remember most about being a little kid. I used to go with my sister and quite often she would go to sleep. There was always a serial— my very favourite was *The Black Whip*. It was just great and you had to go every week or else you would miss the next episode. Of course, you had cartoons and a preview of the coming feature and probably a newsreel. It was funny, because during cowboy movies when guys died, my sister would always think they were dead so we had to sit through the movie again to make sure they weren't. My mother would come and find us asleep in the theatre. She knew where to look. In those days it was safe to go to the theatre with your little sister and walk down the street. We lived a block from the Roxy.

I remember getting my tricycle. It was really solid, really beautiful. I had it about three minutes before I ran into a tree. I loved the swings and especially the teeter-totters. They call them see-saws now. And dodgeball. I remember playing a lot of dodgeball. I remember sitting on Grandma's knee and listening to the radio in the kitchen. Then I remember when we got TV, black and white. We weren't allowed to watch it much. Used to watch "Howdy Doody" and "Maggie Muggins."

Kitty-corner from the school was the outdoor skating rink where we hung out most of our lives during winter, and even in really cold weather we'd go to the skating rink. It had a shack and my most vivid memory is the splintered floors where you go in with your skates and the smell of burning wool on the potbellied stove. Sizzling gloves, wool mitts. Lights, just bare strings of lightbulbs, and they played music. Then, they had a separate ice rink for hockey. That was outdoors too.

In the summer the main thing was hopscotch, double dutch. Everyone used their own favourite clicker. Everybody had autograph books and you'd get people to write in them. I don't know why it was such a big deal. There was always stupid things in them. Most of them started out "Roses are red, violets are blue" and then two stupid lines. Like "If you get mad at me, I'll hit you with a ski." They were always sort of silly little things. "2 nice, 2 be, 4 gotten," remember that one?

I had pen pals, but it never lasted very long as I'm not good at writing. I'd start out with good intentions. And, just like a diary, I'd keep it for three days and that was it. I just didn't like doing that sort of thing.

Every summer we'd go to Vancouver. We went on the train a few times until my mom decided she would rather drive and have a car when she was there. On the train there would be these really nice conductors, the nicest guys. They were just wonderful with kids and they

Candace and a group of friends, in 1957. "My first boy-girl party," she says.

made you feel really good. I just loved sleeping in those berths, they were so cozy and the noise of the train rocking along. My mom would take us to the dining car where they had linen tablecloths and guys in white outfits who treated you like you were really important, and when you're a little kid, that's a big deal, right? We really had to behave. My mother was very strict. We knew if we didn't behave we'd never get to go again. We'd get to Vancouver and for part of the time we'd stay in those beautiful big houses in English Bay before all the big apartments. They had rooms and big verandahs and you'd be within walking distance of the beach. It was kind of a bed and breakfast without the breakfast. Then we would go over, on the CPR ferry, to Victoria. We would visit my uncle who lived in Victoria. My Uncle Albert used to own the parking lot on Yates Street. There was an alleyway you would drive through and he would take your keys. I thought it was such a big deal when he would let me work with him and I'd get to take the keys from the people who were going into the parking lot. Every summer we used to go up to Qualicum Beach and they had these wonderful bungalows right down by the water. They're all gone now. I can remember sitting there with my granny and thinking how beautiful it was. My sister and I would spend the whole day running around on the beach collecting snails and shells.

I used to take the bus downtown by myself—this was a big deal—to the library, get my books and then I'd go to the Hudson's Bay and I'd have a malt and a hot dog because I wasn't supposed to. I never said anything as Dad wouldn't allow us to eat hot dogs because they weren't good for us. Once, in the Bay, I was wearing this blue coat and I fell on the escalator and ripped the hem. The store wanted to phone my parents and get me a new coat but I just didn't want them to do anything, because then my parents would know that I'd been in the Bay and had a hot dog. So I said, "No, no, no, it's okay," and went home with my ripped coat.

On Saturdays in the summer we'd go to the drive-in movies. The snack bar was great. That's the only time we could have junk food—

even a hot dog. And corn-on-the-cob dipped in real butter. My dad used to take us out quite often on Sundays, to Leduc or some town, and we'd go to the hotel for dinner. I think that was to teach us how to act in restaurants.

I loved going to the library. I loved to read books. I read all the Nancy Drew books. She was my heroine, there's no two ways about it. And I loved colouring books. I could colour for hours. I had a red toy box and a rocking horse that my dad made. He used to make rocking horses for the church for families in need. When I was a little kid I would sit down in the basement where he was working. He had made me a little table and chairs and he had bought me a tiny tool set with a hammer and I'd sit there pretending I was making things just like he was. I think my interest in home repairs, which I do a lot of, stems from that. I really wasn't a doll-type person. When my father died, I got all his books on how to make things, and I use them.

▷ **Louise, born in 1947**
   grew up in Slocan, British Columbia

We played marbles in the spring. I can remember using those big shooters: steelies and cat's eyes. In the winter we'd go sleigh riding and build snow forts. In summer, swimming and raft building. And fishing. Of course, you'd have to dig your own worms if you were going fishing. We picked wild strawberries and huckleberries. And at Easter time gathered Easter lilies up in the mountains. Yellow ones, though, not the white ones. Lady Slippers. And Murrell mushrooms.

I played dolls, of course, and played house. I also played paper dolls. We'd cut them out of the catalogue and glue them on cardboard to stand up. And cut out clothes from the catalogue to put on them.

We used to go and watch the Trail Smoke Eaters, a hockey team. When TV first came in, it was really snowy for years. My dad wouldn't get a TV. He said you can't see anything anyway. I think I was maybe thirteen or fourteen (1960-61) before we got TV.

Fifties kids remember playing records on marvelous new record players like this one.

I remember playing records at home, 78s. We had a record player before we had TV. My mom had joined some kind of a record club. "Memories Are Made of This," I remember. Then as we got older, we bought our own 45s.

▷ **Greg, born in 1947**
grew up on the Tsartlip Reserve on Vancouver Island, British Columbia

I hung around with my older brother and we played on the reserve. We went swimming. We used to slide down a hill when the grass was long. We'd flatten it out and slide down. The best friend I had was my cousin. He was a year and a day younger than me. We hung around on the reserve and at school. There's a place down in Brentwood called Moodyville—that was a hangout. We'd get some money. He'd give me his twenty-five cents and I'd still have mine. He was good-natured.

In those days there wasn't much to do, so school added to the activities. We played softball. We played soccer. We got into some running. And of course the big thing was war canoe races, so we travelled to Cowichan Bay, Esquimalt and Bellingham. I guess I was six or seven when I started.

▷ **Thelma, born in 1948**
grew up in Vancouver, British Columbia

Being a small neighbourhood, we grew up almost as in a small town. We had a lot of privacy to make our own entertainment. Even unathletic kids spent a lot of time playing hopscotch, scrub and tag. We walked to the store twelve blocks away to buy a nickel's worth of jawbreakers at three for one cent. Pop bottles at two cents per bottle provided us with our spending money. We had clubs with elaborate rules and only three members. We played forfeits: "Heavy, heavy hand over thy head, what shall the owner do to redeem it?"

Once in a while we would get a group together and put on a show for a captive audience of parents. Singing, dancing and acting inexpertly done and performed wearing costumes of towels and blankets. Refreshments consisted of cookies and Freshie, similar to Kool Aid.

With any luck, we would have some nice sunny days in summer. Then we would recruit a mother to take us to the beach. Almost no one had a car so there was the long walk to the bus, one transfer to the Kitsilano bus and a long day at the beach. We wore our suits under our clothes and carried our underwear and lunch wrapped in our towel—

no plastic bags yet! There was a special way to wrap your towel so nothing would fall out. After a long day in the sun and sea, we would catch the bus home, having changed under the blanket mother brought to sit on while watching us swim.

One of the most exciting times, the Pacific National Exhibition, came at the end of summer. It was the only time we went to an amusement park. We would go to the parade first. Of course that entailed about a one-hour bus ride to downtown. You had to be early to get a good view and the floats and bands seemed to go on forever. There was one girl who was a mascot for the BC Lions and a champion swimmer, and she would walk a good portion of the parade on her hands. When we went to the PNE it was usually on Children's Day I think, for the cut rates. We would not spend the money for lunch but take a tour of the Pure Food Building and sample all the demos. Quite a mishmash but interesting. Our favourite rides were the Tilt a Whirl, the giant ferris wheel and the Shoot-the-Chute that hurtled you down a long chute in a boat-like affair into a big tank of very oily-looking water. What glorious, scary excitement. Then home on the bus, slightly wet.

Sounds like an idyllic childhood but of course there was some darker times. We had bushy empty lots around, and we always were afraid there might be a "bad man" hiding there. And of course because it was postwar, we were given rather unsettling and somewhat ridiculous instructional films about what to do in an air raid and how to put on a gas mask.

Then, before you knew it, the Korean War started. I think I had a lump in my throat the whole time. My oldest sister met and later married a Navy man. The whole household waited with bated breath for his letters to arrive. They came in batches so it was either feast or famine. And like most children, I was worried that the fighting might come to my part of the world.

Another unsettling thing I remember from that time is the McCarthy witch hunts. It seemed every newspaper and news program contained reports of yet more communists. I didn't know what a communist was, but it had to be something really bad for all the fuss they made about it. There was even an early TV show about it called "I Led Three Lives" or "I Was a Communist for the FBI." Each week the hero and his family were almost exposed to the communists. Quite a cliff-hanger.

Family entertainment before television often included playing cards, for me, mainly cribbage which I learned as soon as I could read the numbers. Hearts—my mother played a killer game of that. My older sisters played a lot of canasta and double solitaire but I never got into that. Their friends would show up at the door on a regular basis. Our home was small but very welcoming.

It seems we young children would play the same games obsessively for weeks on end—jacks, bingo, Monopoly (Mother called this Monotonous). I loved cut-outs and dolls and spent most of my time dressing them. Later on a bunch of us spent many happy hours designing clothes for Betty and Veronica and Katy Keene who were *Archie Comics* characters. When we were a little older and with permission, we would walk across the golf course to the Fraser River. It was glorious to watch the tugs towing booms of logs and to wave to the fishing boats coming and going. To this day I am able to ease my stress by watching flowing water.

A couple of times I remember corn roasts organized by the neighbours which took place on the riverbank. The bonfire and the dark combined to make for a thrilling evening for a five or six year old.

Movies were a rare treat and mainly consisted of Disney shows, musicals and comedies. I do remember seeing 3D in Victoria with my sister and brother-in-law. I was sure that lion was coming right into the audience. Any violence would send me hiding under the seat and my family had to keep saying, "It's only a show."

The teenage years were fairly good ones for me. I managed to find a group of girl friends who were respectable, quiet and somewhat studious. We went to all the school dances, got together at each other's house, went baby-sitting, did some bowling, studied together. None of us had boyfriends much of the time. Surprisingly, most of us married by the time we were twenty.

There seemed to be certain rites of passage. For example, wearing lipstick was for fourteen year olds, stockings and garter belts when you were fifteen, formal dresses at sixteen. I think it was good to have something to look forward to. One of the highlights of our young teen summers was going to camp. I went to a camp run by the First United Church in Vancouver. Our days there were filled with crafts, singing, hiking, campfires and generally learning about life. The girls we camped with came from every strata of society. We learned that one girl never took off her blouse to swim because she had scars from beatings at home and we learned that the wealthy girl also could feel unwanted at home. It was a real eye-opener for some of us.

▷ **Karen, born in 1949**
grew up in Victoria, British Columbia

I used to raid the fridge and go feed the hobos down in the field where the Mayfair Mall is now. That would have been about 1955. There was a brickyard there and a grassy knoll where a lot of hobos were. We call them street people today, I guess. Out of work. I was never afraid of them. My friend and I would go there to play and we used to meet a lot of hobos, all of them men. We were never abused or touched in a wrong way or anything like that. A lot of them used to smell funny to me, probably from alcohol. They would be hungry and I would feel badly and go back home and raid the fridge. I took them a whole glass bottle full of milk and cheese and other things like that. I remember giving them pop bottles so they could cash them in.

My brother and I would sneak into the building in the brickyard. It had an elevator. My brother raised pigeons, so we were always sneaking in and going up the elevator because that was a prime place for pigeons to hang out. Of course, I was the guinea pig and had to collect all the pigeon eggs.

One time we got caught. It was very late at night and a security guard was walking around and he couldn't crank the elevator down so he came up and caught us. As a child it seemed very late but it might've been only eight or nine o'clock at night. But it was dark. My father was not a happy camper when we got home.

All of our time was spent in fantasy play: digging for buried treasure, building forts. We spent time scrounging for lumber and bricks for forts. Some of our forts ended up as homes for the hobos.

Because a lot of people didn't have TV, kids used to look forward to the Odeon Club serials on Saturday morning. Hundreds of kids would fill the theatre. It's what everyone did so you weren't seen as corny if you went. There was always some kind of event before the movie, like a yo-yo contest. I remember my brother was yo-yo champ one year. The movies were serials, cliff-hangers that you had to watch the following week for the next installment. Some of the movies were the classics of the thirties and forties. We watched Tarzan movies with Johnny Weissmuller and Tex Ritter and Charlie Chaplin movies.

I used to love fishing. We fished up at Qualicum. Every summer we would go up there. Again, my brother and I used to get into all kinds of trouble. One time we were hunting minnows and the wind blew us off shore and we got rescued by the Coast Guard at five the next morning.

Anne's family has set up camp.

▷ **Anne, born in 1949 in Winnipeg**
grew up in Calgary, Winnipeg, Vancouver, Victoria and Edmonton

Fun was always a big gang of kids. We always lived in a neighbourhood where there were tons of kids. We would go off and play for hours at a time completely unsupervised, and the parents would know where we'd be or they'd know two or three locations where we could be found. We had great fun running off to play out in the wilds. There was always somewhere nearby where we'd go and play.

In Calgary when I was four or five, we lived on what was called the North Hill. It was a new area so there were lots of wide open prairie fields and we'd head off to the prairie fields and just play imaginary, make-believe games as a gang.

In West Vancouver, our house bordered on a big forest that ended where the Capilano Suspension Bridge is. We were on the West Vancouver side of that. I remember playing with my brothers and friends where there were huge overturned cedar logs that would have moss growing on top of them and all kinds of mushrooms and things. There was an old abandoned railroad trestle there which I'm sure we weren't supposed to go near, but had lots of fun playing on anyway. And there was an abandoned railroad car of some kind in the forest too. When we moved to Victoria, it was the beach. We'd head off to the beach.

In Edmonton, it was the ravines. There are ravines all over Edmonton and there were several in the neighbourhood. There was a kind of freedom that was wonderful, just wonderful for kids. It was a secure feeling because there was a lot of other kids. That's not a freedom our children have because we fear for their safety from other adults more than they ever did then. I remember lots of happy times.

Every summer we went camping. It was lots of fun for us as kids. My mother hated it because it was so much damned work! It was my father's job to set up the camping equipment but she had to do all of the food. Of course there weren't easy foods commercially available then as there are now. But even so there were rarely any shortcuts taken so she was expected to produce, and did, the same kinds of meals that she would at home. When we were on a camping trip she was always lugging cartons of food and dishes in and out of the car and cooking on a little camp stove. We would move on a daily basis. For instance, one year we went from Victoria to Winnipeg on a trip to visit the Winnipeg relatives all seven of us, in a car. But we had fun, and I do thank my dad for that. It gave me an appreciation for the out-of-doors.

Toni Home Permanents were all the rage for little girls. My mother was a wonderful mother, extremely solicitous. Because her mother had died when she was nine, after a long illness, she never really had mothering, so she was intent on giving her kids a lot of mothering. She did everything for us. While she herself didn't do a lot of preening—I don't think she had the time— she took the time to always make sure that I was looked after in that way. I didn't appreciate it then but I certainly do now. I remember having these Toni Home Permanents where she would wind my hair in tight little pin curls and then put on this horrible-smelling solution.

Anne sporting the results of her Toni Home Permanent, 1956.

One didn't work very well, so here I was, at age six, absolutely mortified because I had this mass of really, really curly hair, like Little Orphan Annie!

When I was in grades one, two and three in West Vancouver, my best friend was Sally. We had a marvelous time together. The summer after grade three, we moved to Victoria and I was quite heartbroken, and so was she, that we would lose each other in that way. We kept up, with cards and letters. When I was in Edmonton and we were both sixteen and had written a Christmas letter or something, she told me that she was married. I hadn't even gone out on a date! I thought this was just incredible that she was married, that she had a baby. Shortly after that we went to Vancouver for a family vacation and I called her family and her brother answered the phone and said that they were all out at a funeral. It was the funeral of her husband. She was about seventeen years old, with a child, and a widow. At that point, I thought, our lives are going in different directions. We didn't have any contact after that but I always wondered about her.

Fast forward to many, many years later. We have good friends who lived on Mayne Island and we would go visit them a few times a year and they would come and visit us. This friend is a teacher and has two daughters. When they were young they were in day-care with a neighbour woman and we would meet this woman when we went to visit. She had a son the same age as my son so the two little boys would play together. We had met her and her husband on several occasions over a period of two or three years. One time when we were visiting, they were talking about this woman's eldest son being in town for Easter. She said his father had been killed when he was an infant in a mining accident. That triggered my memory. This woman was the same Sally! We had known each other for about two or three years. I called her that night and she came over right away even though it was midnight. We just looked at each other. We couldn't figure out why we hadn't made the connection before. But it was wonderful and we still visit. A friend rediscovered.

▷ **Linda C., born in 1949**
grew up in Calgary and Sylvan Lake, Alberta

We lived in a suburb of Calgary called Bowness. As children we roamed the surrounding hills and picked wild tiger lilies and brought them home to Mom.

My earliest memories would be from about grade one. I remember being a latchkey kid, which in later years has become a negative term, but back then didn't seem to be a big deal. With both parents working, I came home from school alone and I would be the one who opened the house and whatnot. I remember being one of the first kids on our block, about 1955, to have a television set and coming home and think-ing this was really a big deal to watch "Roy Rogers" and "Howdy Doody" and "Bill and Ben, The Flower Pot Men."

My parents were very much into playing with their children. I give my mom credit for the fact she still plays with her grandchildren. My dad cooked breakfast on Sunday and we'd go to church while he was cooking breakfast because my father wasn't Catholic. We'd come home and my parents would play crib after breakfast and then in the afternoon as the roast or chicken was cooking in the oven, we would play card games, a lot of card games with my mom and dad. Rook and Crazy Eights.

I loved paper dolls. You could buy a book with the dolls and the dresses you cut out. I had a Miss Canada doll—this was before Barbie dolls. That would've been about 1955-56. And remember those huge bride dolls? Weren't they beauti-ful? I had one of those. And a pajama bag, an animal that you stuff with your pajamas—mine was a cat. Mind you, I also had a lot of boys' toys, guns and a train as well. We didn't have any boys in our family so I got all the token boy toys. My dad needed boy toys to play with—so I got them.

As little kids, I was about three, my parents had us all decked out in little cowboy skirts and plaid cowboy shirts and cowboy hats. I don't know if that was because we lived in Calgary or what.

About grade five—about 1959—I think, I wore white run-ning shoes, stirrup pants and shag sweaters. Shag sweaters, shag dresses, shag was really in style. Everything was a shaggy material.

Linda C. all decked out in her cowboy outfit.

You had to be just like your friends. I was so jealous of these two girls who had matching shag sweaters and white little furry things that went around the neck. And they matched. I was heartbroken that I didn't have one just like them. Absolutely heartbroken.

▷ **Dennis, born in 1949**
grew up in Burnaby, British Columbia

In those days, Burnaby was not as crowded as it is today. We had a lot of woods to go and play in. Cops and robbers. Cowboys and Indians more than anything else because that's what was on television—the wild west shows. We built tree forts. And played in the woods. There was still a lot of spaces in that area where you could do all sorts of things, daring things like sneaking into an industrial complex on Saturday afternoon when no one's around just to take a look to see what's there. And then running away and not getting caught. We would go swimming in Steel Creek. You can't do that today.

I have fond memories of being taken down to Stanley Park where in those days the *Vancouver Sun* used to sponsor learn-to-swim classes at Lumberman's Arch Pool. And I'd go to the zoo. It was a real heartbreaker two years ago when I was there and saw the zoo was being dismantled. It doesn't exist now for all intents and purposes. What a shame! It was really fascinating, as kids, to be there, to look at all these animals. Looking at a picture of them just wasn't the same.

I remember my sister took me to see a movie when I was five years old. *Hansel and Gretel*. It scared the hell out of me—the witch throwing the children into the oven.

I remember Mother taking me to Woodward's to see Santa Claus. I have a photograph of it. There's this little four-year-old kid just sitting there, not knowing what to do, so shy and a tear coming down his face. My fondest memories of Christmas are from the mid-fifties.

When I was a kid we'd go down to Woodward's to buy shoes and you had to put your foot in an x-ray machine. I think what they were trying to do was show whether or not the shoe was fitting properly. Years later they stopped doing that.

I remember getting my Davy Crockett raccoon hat and rifle. I had a Meccano set, and a notched-log set to build forts with. And I had a 3-D viewer.

If there was one single event that changed everything in the neighbourhood, it was the advent of television. Around 1955 or '56, that's when it started to come in. Coming home from school each day, I remember religiously watching "The Mickey Mouse Club" out of Seattle, Washington, channel five. Because we could get it in those days. That was before cable. In those days everybody had to have a big antenna on their house. It was a neighbourhood of television antennas. I think we went through two or three antennas before we finally got one that would pull in a signal from Seattle. We were lucky. We happened to be in a geographic location where we could get it but in other parts of Vancouver you wouldn't get the signal because it would go over your head. So I grew up with the M-I-C-, K-E-Y, M-O-U-S-E. I had Mickey Mouse ears. I had a cousin who went to Disneyland and I made sure she would bring back Mickey Mouse ears for me. And I think there was some kind of decoder ring I got one time in a cereal box. Of course the prize was always at the bottom of the box so you opened it from the bottom to get the prize first. And Cracker Jacks. You used to get prizes in Cracker Jacks. You don't see much of that any more.

▷ **Dan, born in 1949**
  grew up on a ranch near Lundbreck in southern Alberta

We played a lot of cowboys and Indians, riding bicycles, playing baseball. We listened to a lot of radio. We listened to a country station on radio. Lot of western music. CFCN out of Calgary. I don't particularly remember TV until junior high.

We had a local ski hill and I was on skis by the time I was two years old. It was a community area operation, operated through a lot of blood, sweat and volunteer labour. Another place where the community got together. We used to get a lot of snow, a lot more than I think we do now.

I used to have to gather the eggs from the chickens but I never did milk a cow until I was in my teens. We had horses and I rode a lot. There was a roundup every fall. It was usually a yearly get-together with everyone. The cattle were brought out of the mountains. They were herded out on horseback and taken to a place called Maycroft Community Hall. They were sorted out there and would be shipped back home by truck from there. There was a big supper and dance afterward at the hall.

I do remember a lot of the get-togethers in the community. There would be dancing, mostly square dancing. New Year's Eve I remember in particular. We had a huge kitchen, so they would dance in the kitchen. We had an old record player and played the old 78s. I still have a good collection of those. Old-time dance music, square dance music and big band music and Wilf Carter, of course. Community was a lot more important than it is now.

The nearest church was twenty miles away. That was a major trek in those days.

▷ **George, born in 1950**
grew up in Vanderhoof and Prince George, British Columbia

Friday evenings Mom would tune in the radio for me to listen to some station that played cowboy music. Although I don't really remember much of the songs, I do remember sitting there, listening to them. In the winter, I listened to "Hockey Night in Canada" with Foster Hewitt. He was great. Listening to him was just like being there, watching it. The Toronto Maple Leafs were a winning team and my favourite. At noon on CBC, we always listened to the "Carson Family" as they came in from their work on the farm, had lunch and talked about the day's events and the local news. On the local radio station, CKPG, Jack Corbett read the news for years. Dad bought Mom a hi-fi one year and then we could listen to records. We had mainly military band music and symphonies. Dad had records of the Ames Brothers and Bing Crosby while Mom's favourites were of Vera Lynn and Nat King Cole. Dad wouldn't allow us to listen to the "modern trash" on the radio. Johnny Cash and Elvis Presley were just getting their start in those days.

Smells I remember were varied and seemingly a lot more intense than they are today. The acrid smoke from the coal fire when the heater door was opened to put more coal in or the hot, dry, dusty smell of the ashes coming out. I well remember how the powdery dust from the roads used to just choke me up when I was young and how you couldn't keep it out of any vehicle travelling on those roads. The rich, sweet smells from the soil where a Cat was clearing the willows and poplar and the smell of wood burning after the land has been cleared. The freshness of the air after a summer downpour is another odour that I have fond memories of. And, of course, Mom's baking. Fresh saskatoon berry pie or apple pie—man, there was nothing like it! Or the smell of Grandma's pot roast with the vegetables cooked with the meat coming out of her beautiful old wood stove when we visited there on a Sunday. It was great. I remember how every different house had its own peculiar smell, and stores did too. I guess they still do but I just don't notice them as much as I used to. I remember quite a few stores having the old wooden floors and the proprietors scattering the coloured sawdust on them before sweeping them. The sawdust had wax, disinfectant and a fragrance added to it. The wax attracted dust and I suppose a little of it was left behind in the wood too as it was swept up, leaving the store smelling fresh and clean. I'm always happy to find a store that still has the old edge-grain fir flooring. They are very rare nowadays though.

Back then, too, every night at ten o'clock the fire hall siren went off. It was the curfew signal for anyone under the age of sixteen to be at home. Kids who got into trouble with the law were often paddled down at the police station. It helped a lot of kids get back on the straight and narrow before they got into more serious trouble.

▷ **Bruce, born in 1950**
  grew up in Winnipeg, Edmonton and Regina

I remember having a tricycle that I was passionate about. I rode that tricycle everywhere. We lived in an area of Winnipeg with a large park right behind us. The neighbours had horses and we had some crab-apple trees in our backyard. I can remember feeding the horses crab apples every day until the owner came over and asked us not to do it because they were eating too many.

The area we lived in in Winnipeg was residential but there was a lot of green space and vacant lots. We had all kinds of places to play and build forts. We'd play cowboys and Indians, tag, hide-and-seek. We spent a lot of time out-of-doors. Much more than kids today.

I was petrified of airplanes, and because of the constant anxiety from that era on the news and the newspapers about the Cold War, I remember being absolutely terrified whenever an airplane came over. I was convinced that that was going to kill us all. That stayed with me for quite awhile. I'm still a nervous flyer.

I remember going to a nursery school in about 1954 or '55. I remember the absurdity of an afternoon nap for a bunch of five year olds. Bill Cosby does a great comedy routine on that and I laugh until I cry because it's so true. I remember playing with Playdough or Plasticine. And I had a one-legged teddy bear. I don't know what happened to the other leg.

I remember listening to radio drama. "The Green Hornet." Comedy shows. My parents liked the comedy. I remember a lot of laughter. The radio was on a fair bit in the evening. "Sergeant Preston of the Yukon." That

LPs of radio shows we listened to in the forties and fifties: "The Green Hornet" and "Amos 'n' Andy."

used to scare the heck out of me, especially the wolf howl and that's probably why, to this day, I do not like dogs. I have a passionate dislike of dogs.

My father was a reader. Almost every evening my brother and I would curl up in the big armchair with my dad and he would read to us as my mother knit or mended. I'm still a passionate reader although, interestingly, my brother isn't. My father read a lot of books to us that he must have liked as a boy, or that his father had read to him, because they were from the nineteenth century. Henty books. Two others in particular I remember. One by Captain Marryat, called *Children of the New Forest*, about two children hiding out from Cromwell's soldiers in the civil war and the other one, I'm not sure who wrote it, called *The Settlers in Canada*. It was about a pioneer family from Britain in the 1830s and '40s in Canada. I've often wondered if that didn't start my interest in the past. It was certainly an influence. We'd get a chapter a night. Then we'd have to wait to find out what happened next. I remember being really excited by that.

I remember when television came in. That was a big event. It would have been around 1955-56. I remember the first TV set on the street. A neighbour right across the street got the first TV in the neighbourhood and all the kids went over to watch. I remember going over to their house at about 4:30 every afternoon to watch "The Lone Ranger" and Tonto. We didn't get our own television until a year later.

My grandfather, who passed away before I was born, had purchased some land on the south shore of Lake Winnipeg from an aboriginal nation. He built himself a hunting cabin and he and his buddies would go down every spring and fall for hunting. But in between, my grandmother would pack up my father and his siblings and they would go down to camp all summer. Then when we were growing up, all my father's family would all bring their children to camp. They would coordinate their holidays so that all the cousins, all the families, could come together on the south shore of Lake Winnipeg for anywhere from two weeks to the month, depending on how many holidays somebody had.

In about 1956 or '57, my brother and I got one of those early tabletop hockey games from our parents for Christmas. We played with that thing forever—to the point where it drove my mother crazy. The yelling and the "shush, shush, shush" back and forth—I remember that quite vividly.

▷ **Barry, born in 1952**
grew up in Saskatoon, Saskatchewan

I remember when milk was delivered by horse-drawn wagons. It was a big deal to pet the horse and feed it a carrot or some sugar. Sometimes the milkman would let you and sometimes not. The horses would, of course, leave piles of manure on the street. In winter I recall stick-handling these frozen "road apples" on my way to school. In summer, they would remain in a pile in the street waiting to be cleaned up but I can't remember who did that or how often. As a parent now I can hardly believe that as a kid I would play out on the street with the others, in and around horse manure. Times have changed.

For some reason, I also remember burning barrels. Everyone had a burning barrel in their backyard out by the alley. You could, as I recall, burn your garbage anytime. Then only on Mondays, I think, and finally not at all. But I do remember the smells and the rising smoke when people were burning their garbage. I remember cleaning out the garden in the fall and burning the corn stalks and dead raspberry plants, and the smells associated with all of that. It's hard for me to believe now that such liberal burning was allowed at all, considering all the risks connected with it.

I had a Meccano set and a Tinker Toy set. Want to know something? I still have them! They are downstairs and my kids use them now. There isn't much left from the Meccano and to be honest neither of my kids shows much interest in it. I'm shocked at the price for a Meccano set today. They are around $70 to $100. They do like the Tinker Toys and we have purchased new pieces for it. As a child I showed little interest in either. My mom said all I ever wanted was a ball and a hockey stick.

Perhaps my most vivid memories belong to minor hockey. I played in the old Saskatoon Playgrounds Hockey League. Each school had one team in each age group. If you were not good enough to make that team you didn't play hockey! We've certainly progressed a great deal with our minor sports philosophy. The games were all played on outdoor rinks, imagine! And you had to listen to the radio because when the temperature dropped below minus 10 degrees Fahrenheit, games were cancelled. The first team I played for—John Lake D's—I missed our first game because I was so desperate to make the team that I refused to leave the ice during the last tryout on a bitterly cold night. I froze my ears so badly they both blistered and I spent three days unable to leave the house.

One of the players on that team, and some others as we grew older, was Stan Houston, whose father is Dr. Stuart Houston. Dr. Houston would bring to our games a buffalo robe coat that he owned to warm the players. Each player could wrap it around him for his allotted number of minutes and then Dr. Houston would take it off and move it to the next player. I remember how heavy it was, how it warmed you instantly and how cold it was when removed.

Finally when spring arrived, I remember the inter-school and city marble championships. I don't think anybody plays marbles any more. This was an annual rite of spring and a big deal. Each school declared an age-group champion by virtue of competition within the school on the playgrounds and that champion then advanced to the city playoffs, held annually, I think, at King Edward School.

The marble world had a language all of its own. You couldn't "ever a shooter" and "hunchies" was completely forbidden. Evers meant using your shooter to hit your opponent's shooter so that when it becomes his turn he is at a disadvantage. Fan evers means you can't ever a shooter. Got it? Hunchies meant moving your shooter closer to the marble you were aiming at.

"Rounders," or moving your shooter in a circular fashion to get a better line on the marble you are about to shoot at, might be allowed unless someone before the match declared "fan rounders," and usually it was "knuckles to the ground" when shooting. You either played "funsies" or "keepers" and, to protect your marbles, you could sometimes declare "Chinatown." You always kept track of how many you were up, that is, how many marbles you had won from others. It was like the wild west out there. Eventually the real good players, by virtue of reputation and playground talk, would challenge one another, set the rules and play. It would, at least on our playground, draw a crowd and in its own way help to establish the playground pecking order.

I listened to "Peanut Theatre" on the radio each morning before going to school. As I recall, this was a five-minute-or-so story read each morning on CKOM. I used to take one teaspoon of cod liver oil, listen to "Peanut Theatre" and then it was off to school. Other than that, I don't think radio was a part of my life until my teens and the arrival of the British Invasion.

I don't recall ever getting a television. I just remember always having one. There are four to six programs that I remember watching when I was very young. I remember "Howdy Doody" with Cowboy Bob and the Peanut Gallery. "Flash Gordon," "Forest Rangers" and

"Razzle Dazzle" I would watch after school. "Flash Gordon" was serialized and had terrific story lines. I remember well Flash, Dale and the evil Emperor Ming. I was always envious of the guys in the "Forest Rangers." They had their own fort and

Coca-Cola sign advertising a price of five cents a bottle.

were so independent. "Razzle Dazzle," of course, was a monster hit. I was an official member of the Howard the Turtle Fan Club and even had my own secret decoder to decipher the mystery message each program left you with. Michelle Finney and Al Hamel started their careers there.

"The Mickey Mouse Club" was a tremendous show but I could only watch it when we visited Regina to see my grandparents. Regina was big time because they had CTV and we had only CBC here in Saskatoon. CTV carried "Mickey Mouse." I was in love with Annette Funicello—I probably still am!

"The Terrible Ten," if the title is accurate, was like the "Forest Rangers." It was made in Australia and in it was a character who had a magic boomerang. When it was in the air, "all time stood still" as I remember the voice-over describing it. I was again envious of this boy and his friends who had their own clubhouse and so much independence.

Another big program too was "Hockey Night in Canada." I remember the Saturday night routine was have a bath, watch the third period and have a snack, then go to bed. It was great as I recall.

▷ **Bill, born in 1954**
grew up in Rosthern, Saskatchewan, until 1964

We played marbles, jacks and road hockey with frozen horse turds from the milk-wagon horse. That horse and cart brought the milk each day until about 1961. In the wintertime you'd have to remember to fetch the milk off the step or the cream would freeze.

Summers were more memorable. Because we had relatives who had farms nearby I spent days and weekends at one or the other of the farms. We'd drown out gophers by pouring water down the gopher holes. I remember it as just an ordinary small-town boyhood in Saskatchewan. You could just go wherever you wanted to go, wherever you wanted to roam.

We had huge family gatherings with relatives on my mother's side, four or five households on various farms. At Christmas the weather was always unpredictable—could be a calm nice day or a raging blizzard. There was always the debate. Should we go and take a chance of getting stuck out there on the farm for a day or so? Although I can't remember ever getting storm-stayed.

Work hard, be good and you'll go far

As children, many of us received a weekly allowance that we usually spent on candy and soft drinks. Some of us worked to earn our own spending money for reasons that usually had to do with economic necessity and lessons in self-reliance, in equal measure. Our parents believed in the work ethic and had been taught as children that leisure was generally unworthy of pursuit if not outright sinful. They imparted this attitude to us but probably with less conviction than their parents had.

Those of the fifties generation who started their careers in the fifties entered male-dominated workplaces. Corporate board members, managers and supervisors were almost exclusively men. Workers were expected to adhere to a dress code that dictated that men wear suits and ties and women wear stockings with dresses or skirts and blouses. Only outside workers wore denims and these most often were coveralls.

There seemed to be work for everyone. Although unemployment insurance had been introduced in 1940, collecting it was seen as a less than honourable position to be in and certainly not desirable.

Those of us who started our careers in the early sixties encountered much the same workplace realities and rules. As an adult, my first job after graduation was in an office where good handwriting was a prerequisite of the job. We used manual typewriters with carbon paper to make copies and later produced copies on a cumbersome, noisy and hand-cranked Gestetner machine. Other people did accounting in huge hand-lettered ledgers, aided by manually operated adding machines. Over the ensuing years, these tools of business rapidly evolved so that today we use high-powered copiers and computers for all of these things and much, much more. The computer has been the most pervasive instrument of change in the lives of the fifties generation. It has changed our home, community and work life in incalculable ways.

▷ **Peter P., born in 1935**
grew up on a farm near Winlaw in southern British Columbia

I went to school until 1950, when I was fifteen—I was in grade seven so maybe not even fifteen. I stayed with my mother and helped on the farm for a couple of years and then I went to work logging. And I worked for the CPR for awhile. When I was first logging, I made a dollar an hour. You were lucky to get that kind of money at that time. Later on though, it seemed like it was easier getting work.

When I went logging, I would buy leather-soled shoes and if I needed cork in them I would put it in myself. The shoes and everything would cost less than $20. You could buy a pair of shoes for $12, I think it was, and the cork was a little over a dollar. You'd fill up a little pan of water and soak the soles of the shoes, just soften them up, and leave them overnight and force corks in and when the shoes dried out the cork would stay in. I had to work about two days to earn that kind of money.

When I was still a teenager, I tried to save my money to buy a car. It took me awhile but I did. What else did we spend our money on? Well, we did a little bit of drinking once in awhile. Not really serious. Mostly wine.

My first car was a Pontiac, a 1955. Brand new. $2,500. I had to borrow $500 from my step-dad. But I saved the $2,000. At that time I had a steady job. I was making $1.50 an hour. I got, I think, $200 a month clear. So it took me a little over two years to save that money. There wasn't much to spend money on. Gas was cheap. Forty cents a gallon.

At that time you didn't think too much about divorce. I was originally married in a Russian ceremony, and was later legally married, but we never thought about divorce. It was a no-no. So if you married, you were stuck. So you had to make sure it was the right one.

Back then, I didn't know what I could accomplish. I figured if I kept on working and having a better house, and better this and better that, things would always be better in my life and surroundings. I never believed that I would get this far. I figure that I accomplished more than I ever dreamed of. I dreamed about it but didn't think it would happen. But it did happen. Now I'm trying to retire.

▷ **Jim, born in 1937**
grew up in Pipestone, Manitoba

When I was a kid, I used to go, in the summertime, with my dad painting bulk stations and the pumps. We had a contract with one of the oil companies in Manitoba to go around and paint all the stations and I went with him from the time I was about eight.

I used to work on farms on the weekends, picking rocks, cleaning barns, making hay. And I fired the school furnace for $30 a month for a couple of years. I went down every morning and lit the fires and had to go down again at ten at night and stoke it up again for the night. My mom was the custodian in the school for twenty-some odd years. That's how I got the job firing the furnace. During summer holiday when I was in high school, I worked in the oilfields. In 1953-54, I made about $1.10 an hour.

After graduation, most of the girls got married. Two kids were killed in industrial accidents shortly after getting out of school. A job wasn't hard to get. You worked at whatever you could make the most money at. I went pipelining for a time in the oilfields. I went to work on the rigs when I was about eighteen years old. My dad and I were working together. He had a car and I bought a travel trailer and we lived together. He did the cooking. It was great. I worked on the rigs in Manitoba and eastern Saskatchewan, around Estevan. Then I worked for Carnation Foods at their potato processing plant. Every job I've ever had, I made more money than on the one before. I'm now working as a boilermaker/ welder and I've been doing that for years. The last job I was on was in Powell River. We were building a bleaching tower. Now I have about another year to go and I'm going to retire.

My parents taught me that if you wanted anything, you had to work for it. They never said you couldn't have it. I mean if you wanted something, you worked and went and bought it.

▷ **Elaine, born in 1938**
grew up in the village of Botha, Alberta

Elaine in 1996.

We got an allowance, maybe fifty cents. I cleaned the community hall, that was $2, probably started that when I was about fifteen. And I baby-sat. And then I started once in awhile playing with a band, playing piano. I remember making $10 because this one band's pianist didn't show up and someone said I could play. I had the world by the tail! I bought a pair of high-heeled shoes with that ten bucks and I was so proud of myself.

In the summer holidays, I worked in the kitchen of the hospital between grades eleven and twelve. During grade twelve, I worked weekends in Stettler in a cafe.

As a girl your choices were nurse or secretary or teacher. After high school, I went to work in a drugstore. One thing that just shows the change in attitudes—at the drugstore, we spent hours in the back, wrapping the boxes of sanitary napkins in brown paper. They never ever went out on the shelves as they were.

Later I worked in a hardware store, then I got married. I was eighteen. I fell in love, simple as that—and I'm still in love.

▷ **Gary, born in 1938 in Manitoba**
grew up in Vancouver, British Columbia

I had a paper route for about three years. At that time *The Vancouver Province* was coming out in the afternoon. You'd have your big CCM bicycle with a carrier on the front—I actually had a Raleigh bike with a Dyna-Hub. People remember the Dyna-Hub. The Dyna-Hub was a built-in generator that sat on the front wheel of your bicycle. Some of the bikes had this generator that you flipped over that ran on the back tire to make power. The Raleigh Dyna-Hub was an English bicycle and this generator was on all the time and you just attached wires to it.

I remember delivering papers for *The Vancouver Province*. There was a supervisor and you'd have a paper shack in the back alley behind some stores in the little shopping district. The kids would be standing around and when the paper truck came up the alley or around the corner, the kids would yell, "Rags!" which meant that the paper truck had arrived.

Unlike the boys who lived on the prairies with *The Winnipeg Tribune*, when you got out to Vancouver we learned how to roll the paper. Still can do it to this day. You rolled the paper and you could throw it as you went by the doors and some of us could hit the door, twenty-five yards away, with the paper the way we rolled it. People didn't like it when it banged on the door.

Something else that we did then too, many of us worked in drugstores as delivery boys delivering prescriptions. I worked for a drugstore called Owl Drugs. Every meat market had their meat-market delivery boys. You had to be good to get on with a meat market and deliver meat.

And I was a pin setter. I'd set pins at a five-pin bowling alley. But the ultimate was, well, you'd be considered a super pin setter, one of the best, if you could work the Friday night men's league, from nine to eleven, because you had to be good and fast setting up those pins. We'd get maybe $3 per shift but boy was it good having that extra money.

I quit school early. Back in the fifties jobs were easy to find. You could start one job one day and if you didn't like it, you could start another one the next day. So I went to work in a factory, Simmons

Mattresses in Vancouver, making mattresses and box springs. On piece work. Just a young kid, fifteen years old. Made $135 a month. I thought, This is just absolutely wonderful! I did that job for awhile. I worked for the CPR. I worked in service stations. I worked the graveyard shift. We used to wear white outfits with no pockets.

One time my dad had a brand new Plymouth Regency, a push button automatic. I worked at a Standard Oil station at the corner of Burrard and Georgia in Vancouver. One night I didn't put on the brake and his '57 Dodge rolled down Burrard Street into another car in front of Christ Church Cathedral.

▷ Dwayne, born in 1939
grew up in Brandon, Manitoba

In the summertime I was always up at my grandfather's farm at Benito. My mother had a sister there and I used to go back and forth, and I'd spend the whole summer up there. I rode a horse, herded cattle a bit. I didn't really get involved much with the work. Before the age of twelve I had a paper route. I started that when I was eight and a half or so. So I'd get some money that way, just pocket spending money. During the summer when I was up at the farm I always had to get someone to do it for me, for July and August.

Once the age twelve rolled around, then I stayed in town and worked at the farm machine business with my dad. I worked in the parts department. The following year when I was thirteen, I went into the shipping department. Worked shipping tractors and combines and swathers, balers and that sort of thing. Can't remember before but when I was fourteen, I'd make $100 a month. At that same time, I was in the Army Cadets. They would pay you $100 a summer if you went up to Camp Dundurn near Saskatoon. I refused to go because I could make well over double that working with my dad.

What did I spend it on? Probably cigarettes, for one thing. Everybody smoked a lot in those days. Gas for the car. That came along when I was about fifteen although I wasn't supposed to be driving, but everybody did, as long as the police weren't watching. My first car was a 1932 Buick, bought that when I was fifteen. I'd been driving for Dad since I was thirteen or so because he didn't like to drive. Still didn't have a licence to drive, though. There was five of us guys who had cars when we went to school. Not all of them were fifteen, some were older. I wouldn't take mine to school because I was afraid of getting pinched by the police. Not many going to school in those days that had the luxury of owning a car. There were bicycles, the odd motorcycle.

Of course being attached to the farm, when I was very young, twelve and younger, I had always had the dream of being a farmer. Or at least a rancher. I also had another uncle that lived out in Alberta that we had visited a couple of times. He owned this huge ranch. And I often thought, Well, that's close to farming, I wouldn't mind being a rancher either. Of course, that's as a child. But always in the background as I got older, there was always the farm machinery business and of course I lived and ate and breathed farm machinery. Dad was always talking about it, twenty-four hours a day, whenever I saw him.

I was glad to see the fifties go. I was working very hard, practically all of my waking hours were either work or school. When I was at school I was captain of a ball team or captain of hockey teams or captain of this or that. I can remember the day I quit school. I was just so happy to get out of school. Of course the big thing was peer pressure. They never used the words "peer pressure" at that time, but I know today that's what I was going through. I was certainly glad to get out of that.

I went to work for my dad in the farm machinery business; eventually we ended up being partners. In 1977 we sold out. Dad wanted to get out. The farm machinery business has its peaks and valleys and it was sort of at a peak at that time, and I figured there might be deep valleys between that time and twenty years down the road when the next peak came along. So I got out. On the side I had been playing the organ—nowadays you'd call it an electronic keyboard—and that used to be my hobby and it eventually became my full-time job. I'd started taking music lessons when I was six—on the piano. And I took lessons until I was eight and a half and in grade five, Toronto Conservatory. At that time I quit. There was other things like football, hockey and stuff and I just didn't have the time to devote to it. Then when I was about twelve, I decided to go back at it again but by this time I wasn't taking any lessons. I just took it up by myself. I could read music so I taught myself more or less. And when I was fourteen, I started taking vocal training. I took four years of vocal training. And then there were different choirs that came along, Kiwanis Boys Choir, a church choir.

▷ **Marilyn, born in 1940**
 grew up at Lake Cowichan, British Columbia

My early chores included working at the store doing girl things, filing, doing the books, while my brother looked after the produce stand. We lived outside of town, three or four miles outside of the town, and when I was about thirteen and my brother eight, we'd drive into school with my dad, and work at the store before we went on to school. So we used to work for a bit in the morning at the store, but not every morning. Dad used to go into Victoria every Thursday because the store was closed on Thursday, so Friday mornings were particularly busy because my brother helped him get all these things sorted out while I filed the books and did the paperwork that developed as a result of the trip to Victoria. And I worked in the store on Saturdays.

My favourite thing to do at Christmas time was putting together the Christmas hampers that Dad used to deliver on Christmas Eve. He'd say to me, "Now we have to have a $10 hamper and a $20 hamper," so I'd go around the store putting together things that I thought would be most useful for a family that would amount up to $10 or $20 or whatever it was. And putting together staples and always throwing in some special treat like a can of shrimp or a bag of nuts or something wonderful. At least in my view they were wonderful. Then delivering those with my dad. That's probably my fondest memory of Christmas. We took inventory at the store every New Year's Day. The local vice-principal of the high school used to help my dad do the inventory and so did we kids.

In the fifties the boys in my community had absolutely no trouble getting jobs. They all worked on the weekends at the local sawmill and made bunches of money. The girls had much more difficulty. They might get jobs at the local stores. You were really lucky to have a parent who was in business as opposed to working in the mill or the logging camp when it came to being able to get summer and weekend work.

The year I graduated from high school, 1957, I went to the Shawnigan Beach Hotel to work in the kitchen. I earned $15 a week. I worked six days a week. We got room and board. I chipped ice, made coffee, poured juice, cut grapefruit, all of those kitchen kinds of things. And there was no tips because I was in the kitchen. That fall I went off to university but went back to the hotel to work for two more summers. I eventually graduated into being a waitress in the dining room where I made tips, and I did very well. By 1960 I was probably making $60 a week in the dining room, and doubling that with tips.

▷ **Steve, born in 1941 in Edmonton**
  moved to Williams Lake, British Columbia, in 1953

We got an allowance. And my uncle would hire me for ten cents a day to clean up the suite in his basement. But I had a pretty heavy red licorice habit so that took care of the dime.

▷ **Peter B., born in 1942 in England**
  came to Canada in 1944 and grew up in Regina, Saskatchewan

School was a challenge. I found things more interesting outside school. I seemed to learn better from people than in a classroom. I got a job when I was fourteen delivering groceries with George Little. He owned a grocery store and he and his wife were good to me. I helped him deliver groceries after school and on weekends for about a dollar a day. When I was sixteen and got a licence, he gave me the truck and I delivered groceries while he worked in the store. There were so many people on credit and George let the credit build, allowing that they would pay when they could spare some money. Some deliveries were all the way across the city because they knew they could charge groceries and pay when they could.

By this time I had two sisters and three brothers and money was scarce. I dropped out of school at sixteen. Needing money that my family could ill afford, I went to work at a concrete company loading concrete slabs and cinder bricks by hand—hard, backbreaking seasonal work. I worked hard and the next year I was put on a forklift which made it easier and the money was better. I was making $500 a month with overtime—a lot back in the late fifties. Then a

Peter B. in 1996. (photo by Ingrid Yuille)

friend of mine at the *Leader-Post* asked me if I wanted to get into the newspaper. Looking for an adventure, I applied and got a job as copy boy, dropping my wages to about $160 a month. I worked nights, from six to two in the morning, six days a week. It cut into my social life but I soon discovered my life was in the newspaper and I dedicated myself to it. Like they say, the rest is history. I eventually picked up a camera, found I had a real aptitude and have worked ever since at an occupation I love—news photography. I really found a home with the reporters, editors and photographers at the *Leader-Post*. I owe a lot to many of the newspaper men and women of that time, most of them now dead, who took me under their wing and made me one of them.

▷ **Rupee, born in 1943 in India**
came to Canada in 1947 and grew up in Victoria, British Columbia

In about grade three, my brother and I decided that we wanted to sell newspapers. After school each day I would ride my bike from school downtown to sell newspapers until six o'clock at night and then I would ride my bike home.

We made two cents a newspaper. We bought newspapers at five cents and sold them for seven cents. On the average we made about fifty cents a day. We were on a budget because Mom and Dad didn't want us blowing all our money—so we were allowed to spend ten cents of it and the rest of it we had to bring home. We had two little jars each where we would put the money in, and at the end of the week, we'd count it to see how much money we had. After the first year, my dad opened up a bank account and he showed us how to put money in and we would go to the bank with him. We wanted to buy a bicycle and do all those kind of things but my dad said no. If we wanted a bike, he would buy it for us. But we were not allowed to spend our money because he said we had to let it grow. And then he would invest it for us in Canada Savings Bonds. We would go down with him to clip the coupons and were allowed to spend some of the coupon money. We used to get about $16 every three months, so that was pretty good money.

We spent it doing pretty conservative things, like I can remember buying a hat that I always wanted and a jacket that I thought was really neat. We bought practical stuff. We also went to shows. And we used the money to buy little accessories for our bikes.

I sold newspapers from grade three to grade twelve. By the time I was ready to go to university, I had almost $5,000 saved up. When I went to university I worked for this guy. Well, let me tell you about him. Bill. He was Greek. He had a shop downtown. Actually, he was a bookie. All the kids who sold newspapers would go to his shop and they would give him their nickels, dimes and quarters or whatever. Then he would give them dollar bills. In return, we'd buy a pop and he'd set up a TV for the kids. We'd all sit there and watch TV and have a bottle of pop. He was like a surrogate father to us. My mom and dad never came out to watch us play lacrosse, but he would. He would always watch out for the kids. He never took advantage of them. Like at Christmas, he'd put on a turkey dinner for all the kids who came in. Because he never married, this was like his family.

I can remember one time, just as a gag, after I got my driver's licence, I went to him and said, "Hey Bill, I need a hundred bucks, I'm in a jam." And he turned around and opened his wallet. Pulled out $100 and he put it in my pocket. I said, "Aren't you even going to ask me what it's for?" And he said, "No, I trust you kids. You need it? You pay me when you can." Remarkable man.

I worked for Bill when I went to university. I would go to his shop every day after school from five to six and clean the shop. He would pay me $3 an hour which was a lot of money then. I remember people in the sawmills only got three and a quarter. I used that as gas money and whatever, you know, expenses, going to university.

Bill's still around. I keep in touch.

▷ **Bob, born in 1943**
grew up in Regina, Saskatchewan

I worked at a service station, a Royalite, pumping gas. I earned money to support my real love—buying cars. My very first car was a 1929 Chrysler. I paid $3 for it, all in dimes from my piggy bank. I was fourteen years old. Not old enough to drive, of course, so I drove it in fields. Eventually I left it in a field somewhere, probably ran out of gas. Just walked away from it.

After that one I had a '37 Chev Coupe, a '38 Dodge Brothers, a '40 Ford two door, a '47 Chev coupe, then my very favourite one, a 1947 Mercury convertible. Then a '53 Chev, a '57 Ford and a '57 Chev Bel Air. I drove them, fixed them up. Got maybe a hundred bucks for them. Just let them go. No idea, of course, of future value. Now I smack myself upside the head! If I'd kept those cars, I'd be worth a lot of money.

▷ **John, born in 1943**
grew up in Winnipeg, Manitoba

When I was twelve years old, I started working on Saturdays and in the summer. My uncles had a shop and they made things like flat iron washers, so I used to go there and sort washers and scrap iron. I think I started at about twenty or twenty-five cents an hour. I worked on Saturdays which gave me my spending money. Then in the summer I worked and I would help to pay for my going to school—to a private school. I used to pay half of it which was $55 or something a year. I never had to ask my parents for money from age twelve on, I suppose.

Earlier on we had an allowance. What I remember about that is we used to get fifteen cents a week and then my dad—money was really tight at times—then my dad changed it to two bits every two weeks. Smart man. I don't know if I figured it out at the time or later. It wasn't a lot so probably our allowance ended up being spent on candy bars. I remember saving up for a toy when I was a wee little kid. But I don't remember saving up for big things. Probably just came and went. What I do remember is saving up for my school money. And I remember after I got the money I needed for next year, because I'd be working Saturdays anyway, I quit for the summer. And they thought that was kind of an odd thing to do.

In the summer of the eleventh grade, I worked for Coca-Cola. I think I got $52 a week. Lifting these heavy cases of pop—learning to deal with Jewish and Ukrainian people in the north end of Winnipeg. After grade twelve I worked for Strong-Scott, a sheet-metal shop. Actually I just worked there for the summer. Both these jobs my dad got for me.

And I remember at Strong-Scott they were kind of running out of things for us to do toward the end of the summer. I remember cleaning toilets. Actually you know what my attitude was? Hey, this is neat because this is about as low as it's ever going to go. At that age, it didn't matter to me. I figured, Oh, I'm going up after this. It wasn't as if I thought it was my life's work.

My mother and father were both born in Russia, as were their parents. My grandmother was a widow and when they came over they couldn't get into Canada directly, so they went down through Cuba and Mexico and into Canada that way because you could get in more easily. Security was paramount to my dad. When I finished high school I went to work for Eaton's. I worked there for about a month and it was a terrible place so I quit. He thought that was a bad idea because Eaton's equals security. I thought, I don't want to work where conditions are like that. To him that was not the right thing to do. I wasn't terribly worried about the money. At that age you just go out and look for another job.

In our family your options came down to two things: you could either be a teacher or a preacher. For girls, that meant being a teacher was the only option. Everybody in our family is involved with teaching. Last year I was helping teach computers at my daughter's school.

They didn't want us to go to university because you could lose your faith. You could take Teacher's College and go teach. In fact I started taking teaching at university and soon found out it was definitely not my gift.

I used to play around with radios and, as I got older, decided I was going to go and take electronics at Ryerson in Toronto. I started off taking it by correspondence. At some point, I did one of these loony little "Draw Me" things from this outfit in Minneapolis, and I started taking that course. I didn't last with that. They'd get you to do all this work and they'd send back critiques and the critiques would say, "You're very good." It was not like a class setting where you have a feeling if you are good or not. So that didn't last. But I decided I very much wanted to get into artwork, commercial artwork. I might have done some free-lancing, but I wanted my first artwork job so bad, it didn't matter to me whether I made a lot of money at it or not. I just wanted to do it. My father thought I was going to end up on welfare. Instead I worked for the government—kind of welfare with respect!

In my working career, I went from pasting things onto pages and trying to square everything and line everything up to doing it with computers. Using computers is a whole lot more fun, effective and productive. I enjoy working on the computer. I don't know if I would want to sit and do the paste-up with the wax any more. I think I would tire of that. Technology has really enhanced what we do.

When I first started working for the government, I thought I would be there until I retired. That was fine with me. I liked that. The way it has turned out has been a lot more creative and interesting than I ever would have dreamed. Now, I'm sitting in a little town doing computer work that I really enjoy, doing some writing, some photography, working three days a week. Doing woodworking. Painting on the side.

In my father's generation, if they got a job in a factory, that was good. They would hang in there and work until they could retire. That was it. I feel like I've been really privileged to do a lot more interesting stuff. I've been able to quit a full-time job sooner than my dad ever did. I think it's turned out more creative than I would ever have dreamed of. I would've stayed in Winnipeg forever, and my natural inclination and my security-mindedness would probably have kept me there doing the same thing because I had a good job with the government. I probably wouldn't have moved out of Winnipeg or done anything.

Fifty. That's the only birthday that ever bothered me. I think maybe sixty will—it seems like a big number. But fifty was the only one where I thought that I was getting old. I remember people talking about when you're fifty-two—I don't know why this number sticks in my mind—but they said at fifty-two, people don't want to hire you because you're an old person. Having arrived there, it seems strange because I figure you have a whole lot more to offer than you did way back when. All that experience and the skills you've learned. But people do classify you according to age.

▷ **Lil, born in 1944**
  grew up in and near Nampa in northern Alberta

My sisters and I would get up very early the morning after a dance was held at the community hall, which was located right across the street. Equipped with brown gunny sacks, we'd pick all the beer bottles from the area and drag the full sacks home before somebody would come and steal them from us—which happened more than once. Yes, this kid would hide and wait until they were gathered and the sacks full, until we had done the work!

When we were older we did a lot of baby-sitting and Dad paid my sisters and I for baking—a penny a cookie, five cents a tart, twenty-five cents a cake, iced, and fifty cents per pie. I made a lot of money baby-sitting but it cost me money to bake—everything I burnt I had to pay for—even when I thought I had hidden the evidence by throwing pans and all down the outdoor toilet.

▷ **Linda H., born in 1944**
  grew up on a farm near Marsden, Saskatchewan

We got an allowance—ten cents a week. I didn't buy anything with it because there was nothing to buy, if you can believe it. Everything was bought at the Co-op store in town. There was always a grocery list that was phoned in and my dad picked it up, and we didn't go in to the store. Store-bought treats were not even thought of, not even considered. I think if I had wanted to buy a chocolate bar with my money that would not have been allowed. So I didn't really know what this stuff was. So it just sort of piled up and my city auntie said, "I'll give you dollar bills for all your dimes." But I said, "No, I like my pile of dimes. I don't want those green things." My brother was happy to take her up on it, but I didn't. Pretty weird.

The isolation was incredible. I just couldn't wait to get away from that lifestyle. The women, all they'd talk about was kids and canning. All I saw them do was work. Women just worked all the time. And I thought, My god, I'm too lazy, I'm not going to do this. It seemed so boring. I wanted to go out in the world and travel, be a missionary and do wonderful good deeds. I wished that we were Catholic so I could be a nun. The only important thing for women to be was to get married. If they were going to have a career they could be a teacher or a nurse until they found the right man.

▷ **JoAnne, born in 1944**
  grew up in Dawson City, Yukon

We used to heat our buildings with wood. In the fall my father would purchase several cords of wood and then have it sawed into stove lengths. Starting in the fall it was our job (my brothers and I) to load the wood on the toboggan and make sure there was enough wood in the furnace room to last the night. This task was done every day after school, starting in the fall and ending in the spring.

When the first boat in the spring came around the bend in the river, it would blow its horn, letting everyone know it was about to dock. Everyone would run down to the docks to be there when the boat arrived. It really was a big event. Freight was arriving, people were arriving. A new season was upon us. People dressed in 1898 costumes to meet the tourists, giving them a sense of the past—the Great Gold Rush. My friends and I made souvenirs to sell to the tourists. We made little change purses, wallets, canoes, etc., out of birchbark. We burned the word Dawson on them. We would go to the dock to wait for the boat to arrive. We would sell our trinkets to people as they were getting off the boats. We also set up little juice stands and sold drinks. That supplied us with a little spending money.

We used to crawl on our bellies underneath the wooden sidewalks to find money that people had dropped down between the cracks. This could sometimes be very profitable as we would find quarters and fifty-cent pieces, sometimes even paper money.

All of us worked in the store off and on. We got an allowance. I remember getting fifty cents a week and that would get you into the movies. When tourism first started coming to Dawson, I worked at a little visitor information booth for the summer. I was probably thirteen or fourteen at the time. I worked a couple of hours a day. Made a little spending money. I think I made about fifty cents an hour.

▷ **Denise, born in 1944**
 grew up in Regina, Saskatchewan

I started carhopping at Oscar's Drive-In when I was twelve or thirteen. I remember I went for an interview and then went back out to the car and was having a milkshake and they came out and hired me. I started that night. Of course the uniform didn't fit, the pants were too long. The uniform was orange, black and white. When I was fourteen I went to Dog 'N' Suds where the uniform was black pants with a red cummerbund and a red jacket, a white blouse and a red hat, like those old air force hats. You put your hair up underneath, of course. We didn't have runners like now, so we had some kind of black shoes.

The first night I worked, within an hour of starting, I served a convertible and they had ordered four milkshakes, which would be served in what we know now as the large A&W mugs. They also ordered four root beer, four hamburgers and chips and whatnot. A full tray. I backed out of the place where we picked up the orders, and the wind caught the door, the door caught the tray and, in trying to balance it, I ended up dumping the tray into the convertible. So I didn't get paid for the first two weeks because my pay had to cover the dry-cleaning and cleaning the car. Anything that was stolen or broken you had to pay for.

Part of the job was cleaning the toilets, hosing down the driveways and the building, pushing stalled cars off the lot, washing dishes and occasionally cooking because there was only one cook. And you did all that for eighty-five cents an hour. But I made good money in tips.

We had RCMP recruits in Regina and you knew when they came to the drive-in. They had short military haircuts and, of course, the ducktail was the rage then, and they were just so different. The odd time, there'd be a rumble—people coming from out of the area and causing trouble, but that wasn't usual.

Cars were a lot bigger then. Many had running boards. One time I had stepped up on a running board to get a tray that was hooked to the window, and as I stepped off, the car backed up and the front bumper caught my leg and sent me and the tray flying. I wasn't hurt, bruised but not hurt. All I was concerned about was that my hat had come off and my hair was showing. Everyone was so concerned about if I had been hurt and all I could think of was I had to get my hat back on to hide my hair. That was a rule. Keep your hair covered.

I'd go there to work after school about four-thirty or five and work until the place closed at one. We'd work cleaning up until just before two and then the owners would drive us home. Getting up to go to school in the morning was tough. So I took wake-up pills. I worked at Dog 'N' Suds until I was sixteen when I got married. By that time I was head carhop.

▷ **Giuliana (Julia), born in 1944 in Italy**
came to Canada in 1953 and grew up in Michel, British Columbia

My mom died when I was fourteen. By then one sister was married and had two girls, and the other one was in Calgary. I had to stay home and cook, clean, watch my dad, my older brother, my younger brother and the baby. I got the lovely chores.

I wondered what it would be like to go out and have a good time, to go to a dance, to a prom or to finish high school or go to university. Everybody else had the chance to do it, but I didn't.

I did that for a year and then when I was sixteen, I got married and moved to Calgary. He was a welder. Worked on the pipeline. He was a cousin of my brother-in-law. He was twenty-nine. But my dad said if he's a good provider and will look after you, that's the main things. I actually started living after I got married. My husband took me out. We went on trips. He took me to dances. I actually grew up with him. He was really good that way.

I had my babies at nineteen and twenty. And then my life was the kids.

▷ **Anita, born in 1946**
grew up in Vancouver, British Columbia

When I was twelve, I could baby-sit and earn twenty-five cents an hour for the three brats, as well as for doing a day's worth of dirty dishes and bathing them all before bed. Sometimes my pay would increase by ten cents an hour if their parents stayed out after midnight.

▷ **Ed, born in 1946**
grew up in Saskatoon, Saskatchewan

I remember getting a dollar a day for working on the farm, that was like a full day of farm work. I got an allowance, quite small, you know twenty-five or thirty-five cents. I remember it being raised from fifteen to seventeen cents. I remember that. We'd go to movies. At that point in time there was the Children's Film Series in Saskatoon. It was an attempt by some east-side ladies to bring in good movies. I remember buying a subscription to that and going to watch all these movies.

We also had a store out at the farm, a general store. I remember if you had a nap, then you could go and have a coke after. I remember Orange Crush and Cream Soda.

In high school I had no intention of going on to university. My grades in high school would vary from being just-about-asked-to-leave to the honour roll in the same year. So I think my grade twelve average was something like 60 percent so I couldn't get into university. Didn't want to go anyway. I started working at the bank making $2,900 and eventually made $3,100—that's a year. I remember the bank manager at that time, he got to live above the bank, and this was in a small town in about 1964, and he made $12,000 a year, and I remember thinking to myself, How does a man spend that much money? I could never imagine spending that much money. So I went to work in the bank and in about three hours I realized work probably wasn't my forte and I wanted to go back to school. I stayed out a year and took a couple of classes and got a minimally acceptable average to get into university. I went to university for seven years.

▷ **Gail, born 1946**
grew up in Prince Rupert, British Columbia

My first job was clerking in a hardware store in Terrace when I was fifteen. It was an old hardware store in an old, old building with those oil-soaked creosote floors that you put Dustbane on. I earned seventy-five cents an hour clerking there.

▷ **Sandy, born in 1946**
grew up in Winnipeg, Manitoba

I was being raised for some sort of career. I was supposed to practise piano and get good grades. Even my mother's mother was like that. Her husband died when my mom was four so the family kind of ended up separating all over the place, boarding out. All she could do was go and live in and cook for families. So she thought it was a high value to get an education and not be dependent on anybody. So that is what I got.

Later I just kind of wrapped my dreams around whatever my boyfriend wanted, to tell the truth. Because it seemed to change from boyfriend to boyfriend. My last boyfriend was in chartered accountancy. I just thought I'd be the wife of a chartered accountant.

▷ **Candace, born in 1946**
grew up in Edmonton, Alberta

I had my own little garden and I grew lettuce in it the first year. I remember this very clearly because this was when I got my very first allowance. I was really young. And I got twenty-five cents. And I thought I'd died and gone to heaven. So I took my twenty-five cents allowance to the store and I bought a loaf of bread. And I came back and I made lettuce and sugar sandwiches for all my friends—because I had the lettuce in my garden.

I had a bank account when I was little. I used to save quite a few of my quarters from my allowance. I had a little bank book. Banks were so nice to kids. Where could you go now as a little kid and say, "I want to put twenty-five cents in my account." They'd always do it for you. And they'd smile and say, "Boy, you've got $3 in there now!" That probably encouraged kids to save. A trip to the bank was cool.

▷ **Ken, born in 1947 in Victoria**
grew up just outside Edmonton, Alberta

When we were really young, we got a nickel or dime allowance. All of us pretty well earned our own pocket money from the time I was seven or eight. In the wintertime, I shovelled walks and, in the fall, raked leaves. If you got a dime for shovelling a walk, you were doing pretty good. We had paper routes, and I worked on local farms in the summertime. Mostly I spent my money on candy and comic books. When I got a little older, I'd spend it on going to the public swimming pool, the bowling alley, that kind of thing.

Later, when I was in high school, we had a pretty high drop-out rate because of the oilfields and the pipeline. A kid could leave school at grade eight or grade nine and get a $2-an-hour job, which was big bucks in those days. You could quit three jobs in a week and find another one around the corner.

▷ **Louise, born in 1947**
grew up in Slocan, British Columbia

We used to get an allowance. Well, we didn't always get an allowance but if we wanted something then my dad would say, "Okay, this is your allowance." Like if you went to the show, then you got fifty cents, if I remember right. It cost twenty-five cents to go to the show, then you could buy sunflower seeds and pop or something for the other quarter. I used to clean for people, when I was a teenager. My girlfriend and I, we'd clean the teacher's house. I don't know what we got, maybe a dollar an hour. And we baby-sat. I remember when my girlfriend and I were probably ten or eleven. We'd done some work and earned some money so we bought a brick of ice cream and ate it all. I got so sick.

Mostly I saved my money for Christmas presents or to buy particular clothing that I wanted. Most of the time my mom made my clothes. Whenever I got a chance, at Christmas time or whatever, I'd con them into buying me a Christmas dress. I remember one that looked something like a square dance skirt bottom and just a plain top. It was in tiers. It was just plain green broadcloth with ribbing along the tiers. But everybody thought that I was dressed to the nines. The people that couldn't afford to dress their kids that well would say, "You dress her like a doll." I would go with my mom to town, to Nelson, and we'd pick out a flour sack the colour that I wanted, and that would be my dress. She made her own patterns.

I worked in a cafe. I made nothing. I worked for this lady. She said, "Well, I'm not going to pay you right now but you come back around closer to Christmas and I'll give you your money." We went to Nelson, I think, once or twice a year. And at Christmas time, of course that was a major one. And I went to her and asked her if she'd mind paying me and she said, "I thought you enjoyed working here." So I never got paid. I'd worked there off and on for about three years from the time I was twelve.

Actually, at one time I wanted to be a stewardess, and then I ended up having to get glasses so that sort of threw that out. Then I remember I wanted to be a policewoman. Don't know what ever happened to that idea. I just went to grade ten. I left school and worked in a cafe. I worked cleaning houses for people. And then when the hotel came in to Slocan, I worked there. As a waitress. Then I moved to Ladysmith for a year and I worked for Sweet Sixteen in Nanaimo. And worked for Sweet Sixteen in Nelson. Then I went back to the hotel in Slocan to work and that's where I met my husband. I got married when I was twenty-two and we went to Calgary.

▷ **Greg, born in 1947**
grew up on the Tsartlip Reserve on Vancouver Island, British Columbia

We were occasionally given twenty-five cents, which was a lot of money. When our parents were in good spirits, they gave us fifty cents. When I was nine or ten years old, I started picking berries. I can remember we all went to this place in Washington to pick strawberries. There was this big camp. Old cabins, old gas stoves and coal oil lamps. There was people there from all over. From the Island, from all over the province, and some Mexicans, too. We'd spend anywhere from two weeks to a month picking berries. We never knew how much we made. We just picked the berries and made money for our parents. My father worked in the coal yards and when he got laid off each year, we went directly over there. He always worked.

▷ **Linda C., born in 1949**
grew up in Calgary and Sylvan Lake, Alberta

Every Saturday afternoon, we went to the picture shows. The show was twenty-five cents and you'd get a pop and a bag of popcorn for another ten or twelve cents. We got an allowance, maybe a quarter or fifty cents a week, some high-priced amount like that.

I didn't actually get a job until I was in high school. I started working in about grade eight or nine. I baby-sat, especially in the summertime in the cabins. Twenty-five cents an hour for baby-sitting umpteen kids. But my first job, and this was in 1967, I got seventy-five cents an hour. I worked in the grocery store. That was a big wage.

Right from an early age I was going to be a schoolteacher. When I got into high school and thought about what possible career choices there were for me as a female, I realized I could become a teacher, a nurse or an airline stewardess. Those were the only three career choices that were there—that I remember. I was too tall to be an airline stewardess—you couldn't be over five foot eight. Five-ten was too tall. Otherwise, I probably would've become an airline stewardess. I didn't want to become a nurse because I wasn't big on biology and I never liked dissecting animals or blood—it was just not my career path. So teaching was it.

▷ **George, born in 1950**
grew up in Vanderhoof and Prince George, British Columbia

If we had a cent back then, we could buy a bubble gum or one or two candies. If we had a nickel, we could buy a Wagon Wheel or a small chocolate bar. If we had a dime, it could be a bottle of pop, a box of Cracker Jacks, a big chocolate bar or a bag of Cheezies. If somehow we got hold of a quarter, well, the possibilities were so varied that we could treat the whole family to something. I don't remember very often having a few cents though. If the tooth fairy came or we were at a birthday party and happened to get a dime or a nickel in our piece of cake, well, that was really something.

The Orange Crush that came in those brown-glass ribbed bottles, though, was really something. We also had Kik Cola and 2-Way, which we don't see any more. As kids we weren't allowed to have Coke. I was at a flea market the other day and was delighted to see one fellow selling old pop bottles. He had some of the old Orange Crush bottles. He even had 2-Way bottles. I didn't see any Kik-Cola bottles though. And last summer, I found the neatest place. The communities of Sinclair Mills, Longworth and Penny! If the sawmills were running and the old stores with their gas pumps were still in business, it would feel just like home again. I was just delighted to find that area. The houses for the most part have been kept up so they really have the fifties look about them still.

I think my older brother had a paper route for awhile back then, but us younger kids had no real source of income unless a neighbour gave us a nickel to run to the store for something. We all had our chores but getting paid for them never entered our minds.

Kids, being kids, we got our socks pretty dirty sometimes going without slippers or running outside. Mom had the cure for that too. She got out the scrub board and the Sunlight bar soap on washdays and we learned how to use them. She taught us how to darn and iron too, not that she made us do a lot of it. She just wanted us to know how to do these things for ourselves. She taught me how to use the old treadle sewing machine too. None of us knew then that she'd be leaving us in mid-1961 because of cancer, but she sure did her best to teach all of us all she could, before then.

▷ **Bruce, born in 1950**
grew up in Winnipeg, Edmonton and Regina

Mom would always shop on Saturday and we would usually get a treat. Sometimes you might get a nickel or some pennies to get some penny candy. But I don't remember having an allowance. I could always go to my parents if there was something that I needed. Didn't always get the money because it was their choice but I never really had my own money until I started working as a teenager.

I don't remember spending a lot of time thinking about what I would do when I grew up. When I did, it was the usual boy sort of thing. I'll be a policeman, I'll be a fireman. But I don't recall it being a major issue until we got to our teens and then I think, understandably, you start turning your attention to, Well, school is almost done, now what am I going to do? So much of our thinking in that sort of vein revolved around school. And it was just getting through until the next summer.

▷ **Barry, born in 1952**
grew up in Saskatoon, Saskatchewan

I still live in Saskatoon. I teach math at Marion Graham Collegiate. I coach basketball in the winter, baseball in the summer and holiday with the family in our trailer.

▷ **Audrey R., born in 1953**
grew up on a farm near Pelly, Saskatchewan

When I was a kid I toyed with a number of different things I'd like to be when I grew up. Of course, they were girl things like secretary or hairdresser, teacher, nurse, even a lab tech. A friend of mine and I thought for awhile that we would like to be psych nurses. So we went to Weyburn one day to the Psych Centre. Only took us an hour or two there and we knew we didn't want to be psych nurses after all.

The good old days?

The 1950s were our days of childhood innocence. We remember, as every human generation does, the decade of our childhood as the most ideal of our lives. We easily forget the negative aspects, or if we do remember, the sadness fades more as each year passes and we remember the good times, often reshaping the remembered events, consciously or unconsciously, with each telling.

We children of the 1950s are now in our forties and fifties. Midlife. Most of us have children, many have grandchildren. We have grappled with the joys and sorrows of life and now realize that we are older—and wiser. We have reached the stage of life when looking back is sometimes more comfortable than looking ahead. We have experienced changes in all aspects of our life. Our attitudes have changed. Our bodies have changed. Our way of life has changed.

Many of the women of our generation were the first to seek careers in the workplace in large numbers. We remember the transition many of us experienced, from the acquiescent female worker to the assertive, successful manager. The workplace changed. We changed. Some of the women of the fifties generation forged more equal relationships with their partners than their mothers had, while others maintained the status quo. But in the forging of this new reality, there was a cost. Separation and divorce, which were comparatively rare in the fifties, became an all-too-regular part of our reality.

In most instances, the men of the fifties generation were nurtured, too, in a far different reality than the one they live in today. While most of their fathers participated only marginally in running the home and nurturing their children, the men of the fifties generation have adapted as their world changed. With the increasing numbers of women in the workplace and in more senior positions, most of these men have accepted a new reality. They learned to share wage-earning as well as home and family responsibilities with their partners.

Generally, we have been able to afford a more affluent life than our parents enjoyed. With more leisure time available to us than adults only a generation before us, we have had time to more closely examine our role in life, to try new approaches to work and play and to explore the wider world through travel and technology. We invented, adapted and contributed to our world in ways that, as children, we could not have imagined.

Did we bring all of the positives of our fifties childhood with us into adulthood and leave all of the negatives of the decade behind? Obviously not. In looking back, we can now see what we think should still be a part of our lives today and what was best left in the past.

▷ **Peter P., born in 1935**
grew up on a farm near Winlaw in southern British Columbia

Somehow I don't think I'd really want to go back to the fifties. We didn't have a telephone, didn't have power. And you had to work a lot harder to get what you wanted. It didn't seem like it then but now, looking back, it was a problem. But everybody was the same. Some might have had a little more but some would have a little less. They didn't have anybody to compete with, if you know what I mean. I think maybe in some respects people were a little closer. You had time for people. Now you're always busy, there's not enough time.

I remember I used to try to hide from my mother or else she would put me to work, and she used to say, in Russian, "You won't be carrying on your shoulders what you learn. Whatever you learn now takes it off your shoulders later." And she was right.

▷ **Jim, born in 1937**
grew up in Pipestone, Manitoba

The thing that they should have kept from the fifties, as far as I'm concerned, is responsibility. There isn't any any more for anybody, in government, kids have no responsibility, the parents have got no responsibility. That's as far as I'm concerned, and I don't think I'm too far wrong.

There's too many lawyers. Every time they make a new law, it's for the lawyers to make more money. You see people doing things and going to jail for a couple of years and they should never get out. The laws have changed and not for the better, as far as I'm concerned.

Everybody worked then. That's one of the things that should have been brought forward from the fifties. Everybody had a job, which they don't any more. Some of them don't want one and some of them can't get one.

▷ **Elaine, born in 1938**
grew up in the village of Botha, Alberta

It was a wonderful time to grow up. We didn't have a lot of money or anything. Yet I never felt it was tough. I don't think we could've imagined what changes would happen in our lives.

▷ Audrey H., born in 1941
grew up on a farm near Strongfield in south-central Saskatchewan

Audrey H. celebrating her birthday in 1996.

Family values have certainly deteriorated with Mom and Dad working and children involved in so many things like hockey, baseball, Scouts, Guides, band. There just isn't time for a family to be together for quality family time. Divorce adds to the problem. The respect for any form of authority, be it teachers, parents or the law, has been lost in our "me" society. Too many parents are selfish and have no idea where their children are or what they're doing. In the fifties, Dad was the out-of-the-home worker and Mom was always home for and with the children.

We left behind compassion and caring for our neighbour and fell into the materialistic trap of keeping up with the Jones's. So the main things missing today are family values, respect, compassion, caring, friendliness.

I was never in a position to think that women were treated any different than men. Our school had more women than men teaching. Our doctors were male but the nurses were all female. I guess when I graduated in 1959 the choices even then for females were teacher, nurse or secretary as careers, although one of my female classmates took music and another commerce.

Family problems were kept secret then, such as physical and sexual abuse, so the opening of those closed doors has certainly advanced from the fifties.

▷ Steve, born in 1941 in Edmonton
moved to Williams Lake, British Columbia, in 1953

The thing that was the best about the fifties was that you had Mother at home. When you came from school, Mom was there. We had no television and we made our own activities. Out of it came self-esteem.

▷ **Peter B., born in 1942 in England**
  came to Canada in 1944 and grew up in Regina, Saskatchewan

Back in the fifties, everybody had the opportunity to get a job. You didn't have to finish school. Education wasn't as important as it is to-day. And back then, you didn't know what was going on in the world. What you did hear, well, it just seemed so far away and not a part of your life. Today Yeltsin has bypass surgery and we know about it and wonder how that might affect us. A crop failure in Brazil? You hear about it and know that the price of coffee will go up at your corner store. Today I think sometimes we know too much about what's going on. We're bombarded with information and sometimes it's hard to know what's important and what's not.

Back in the fifties, we wore suits to the office—suit, tie, white shirt. Didn't matter how low in the company you were, you wore a suit. Today, society is recognizing people by what they can do rather than what they look like. You can grow your hair long and dress really casually and still be an accepted producer in the company. You sure can't tell by their appearance what their take-home pay is. I think this attitude, and of course technology, allows for much more artistry in the workplace. People don't have to put on a false front like they used to. For creative people, the nineties are certainly a better time to live than the fifties.

I think, at this age, I'm beginning to put things more in perspective than I ever did before. And I do believe in fate—that there is a purpose after all for all of our experiences, good and bad.

▷ **Rupee, born in 1943**
  came to Canada in 1947 and grew up in Victoria, British Columbia

What would I like to see come back? Family values and having the freedom for kids to be kids. And not have to worry about pedophiles and all these other horrible things that are happening. I wouldn't dare think of sending an eight- or nine-year-old kid into town on his bike to sell newspapers like I was able to do then. At that time everybody trusted everybody. There was always a sense of community spirit, and I think there were fewer evil people around.

Everybody's out for me and nobody's out for us. I really believe the family has broken down in a very serious manner. I think maybe we got too affluent, too quickly. Sometimes affluence leads to arrogance and a little too much independence.

▷ **John, born in 1943**
grew up in Winnipeg, Manitoba

One of the most basic things we left in the fifties was a respect for authority. That's disappeared. There was a shared belief that people had in those days, not only in immediate authority but an ultimate authority which I think is missing these days. For instance in those days, if what is coming down the tubes on television this fall had appeared on somebody's screen, 99 percent of the people would have said this is sewage. Nowadays half the people will watch it. Our value system has changed drastically.

Now, many people do not believe there's a God so values are made up. You either make them up yourself or you pick them up from society or whoever. For the standards that are set do not come from something that people in general recognize as the ultimate truth. When they take evolution out of everyday education, it takes God out of the picture. And if you take God out of the picture, then your standards have to be set somewhere else. Could be Carl Sagan or David Suzuki or television or the Supreme Court or the government. If it's any of those things, even the Supreme Court, values will continue to change. The Supreme Court makes decisions quite differently than they did thirty or fifty years ago. There is no standard that people hold to. If we are all evolved from primordial soup, then the value of the person decreases drastically. Things like abortion, I think, are a natural outcome of believing that we are just a bunch of cells stuck together. Human life has a lot less value.

People in our generation are much more likely to share their feelings and affections. In my upbringing there was very little hugging, very little saying, "I love you." People do that much more readily these days with their family. I think that's a whole lot better than it used to be and I think even the generation before us, they're doing it more now than they did. My mother will say "I love you" a lot easier than she did when I was growing up. That's too bad that it wasn't part of our basic upbringing.

What else have we left behind? In those days, if you didn't smoke, didn't go to theatres and dance and went to church, you would then be classified as a Christian. That opens the door pretty wide open for hypocrisy. Nowadays, more people realize it is not based on keeping a bunch of rules, it is to do with relationships with God and with other people. In those days it was a whole lot easier to play the role and get away with it.

▷ **JoAnne, born in 1944**
grew up in Dawson City, Yukon

What I remember most was everybody had respect. There wasn't any vandalism. We didn't have to lock any doors. We respected all of our friends' parents, and would never have dared talk back. We knew what was going to happen to us if we did something wrong. For every action there was a consequence, and we were responsible for our own actions. I can remember playing ball on the street and accidentally hitting the ball through a window, and I had to go and apologize and pay for it. There wasn't any hesitation. That's the way it was. I think there's a total lack of respect all around today.

What of the fifties do I feel should have been left there? I am very glad that ribbed brown stockings and bloomers were left behind, along with the girdles that our mothers thought we should wear when we started to take shape.

▷ **Giuliana (Julia), born in 1944 in Italy**
came to Canada in 1953 and grew up in Michel, British Columbia

I'll tell you one thing, I wouldn't change the fifties because the closeness we had in the family in the fifties does not happen now in the nineties. Family values seem to be drowning.

▷ **Anita, born in 1946**
grew up in Vancouver, British Columbia

There was a kind of carefree openness to everything, back in the fifties. Of course, I was just a kid then. Maybe that's why I remember things the way I do.

▷ **Ed, born in 1946**
grew up in Saskatoon, Saskatchewan

I think one of the things that many of the fifties kids would have typically experienced was that their parents had lived through the Depression. In many ways they had to be much more resourceful and responsible. In many cases you had parents who experienced real adversity and they taught the value of hard work. They also didn't have the resources to spoil their children. I think one of the difficulties now is so much is given and so much is expected as a right. I don't think there's any advantage in thinking that something will come, not as a result of you having done something to get it.

As a Catholic family I can remember doing the rosary damned near every night! We would go on picnics on Saturday to the Forestry Farm and do things as a family because there was very little else to compete. It reinforced the family unit and one's self-reliance. You couldn't go through life then as you can now as a voyeur experiencing life second hand. If you wanted a life, you had to have a first-hand life.

I don't remember much of what was going on then and I must have been totally oblivious to the world. I remember things like the flooding of the Saskatchewan River every spring but I don't remember having any recognition of the world and its implications until high school. I remember going to the other side of the river when I went across the Broadway Bridge. I remember going to the Forestry Farm and we had to go through Nutana. The world kind of paled in comparison. My horizons were west-side Saskatoon and the farm. That didn't stop me from understanding as much or more about the world now than most people. I don't think you have to get everything at all times. In many ways, I think it might have been an advantage.

▷ **Sandy, born in 1946**
grew up in Winnipeg, Manitoba

What did we leave in the fifties? The innocence, the charm. And things were much more black and white.

▷ **Candace, born in 1946**
grew up in Edmonton, Alberta

In those days you always felt safe. You didn't have to be frightened to go anywhere. There wasn't anybody saying, "Oh be careful, don't do this, don't do that." You could walk a few blocks in the evening and not have to be terrified. You know, you could walk your girlfriend halfway home and you never had to worry about it.

The best thing about being a kid is that you don't have responsibilities. I think kids have more to be frightened of today, but I think they still don't have those responsibilities, so as long as they are protected, I think they still feel pretty good. I think it's probably different now, because you have to worry all the time about where your

kids are. In those days parents worried about you, but there wasn't the
things out there that there are today.

I think I must have had a pretty
happy childhood because I didn't
think there was anything that bad
about the fifties. I enjoyed myself.
My parents were good to me. They
took us on trips. We really didn't
want for anything. We weren't, you
know, rich. We were comfortable.

Candace in 1996.

▷ **Ken, born in 1947 in Victoria**
 grew up just outside Edmonton, Alberta

I spent one summer at a YMCA camp for juvenile delinquents because
I'd stolen a bicycle. Just because I wanted it. But here's the difference.
I was fourteen years old, I stole a bicycle and I got a year's probation
with all kinds of conditions. I didn't dare not abide by those conditions. One of those conditions was that all during the winter I had to
be at the YMCA every Wednesday night for a counselling meeting.
Then I had to spend six weeks of my summer at the YMCA camp on a
lake west of Edmonton and take counsellor training. They turned me
from a little bicycle thief into a camp counsellor. Not like today—you
get fifty hours of community service which nobody enforces. It was
positive reinforcement. You had to pay for what you did wrong. Instead of writing me off, they said, "We're going to turn you into a
leader of people—turn you into a camp counsellor where you're going
to teach values to young kids." And I did.

Our generation, the "me" generation, we got too much. We turned
into a very selfish generation. Too much affluence. Too much independence. During the sixties, too, you could do pretty well anything
you wanted. Parents stood around confused, probably like their parents were, but everything was happening too fast—television,
communications, the education system breaking down. At school there
were no consequences for bad behaviour. I'm not a great believer in

corporal punishment but there are certain things that have to have certain consequences. Today, you suspend a kid from school, he tells his parents, and there's trouble.

We grew up with a whole different set of values. There were fights at school but they were broken up pretty fast. If, for example, somebody had pulled a knife at school, it would've been headlines for weeks. The individual who pulled a knife would've been crucified and ostracized socially—at least in the area I grew up, which was a pretty rough neighbourhood. You just didn't pull knives, it wasn't civilized. Today we need to say as a society that we won't tolerate this.

In Alberta and Saskatchewan in those days, there was no real total urban society. Everybody was tied in some way to the land. I can't think of a kid I grew up with who didn't have some relative who they didn't spend some time with on the farm in the summer, or had just moved to the city from the farm or still had acreage and kept horses and chickens and cattle. You didn't have that truly urban generation until the seventies—they grew up in cities and never saw a live cow. Anytime you're closer to the land, you're closer to the elements, have more respect for life and how it's lived. For my whole generation, that was part of it.

▷ **Louise, born in 1947**
grew up in Slocan, British Columbia

One thing I miss about the fifties was the compassion that people had for each other. Today everybody gets too busy with their own thing. People made time for each other then. And I think that came from the war years and the thirties. Everybody had to help each other because nobody had anything in those days. Now everybody wants too much.

It would've been pretty hard to imagine back then that life would be like this. Good or bad. I remember when I was about five years old and we took a trip to Seattle—that was a major trip. Our world was pretty limited.

Being brought up in a small town with the parents that I had, it made me watch my dollars a little. But that doesn't say that's how it was with everyone. It all depends on how you looked at things when you were brought up. But you were taught to appreciate things, whereas today it's, "How many more of those can I have?" not, "Gee, I've got one. Is that ever neat?"

I don't really have too many bad thoughts about those days. People appreciated things more. It would be really nice to see the fifties back again. It wasn't that hard a times that I remember, as a kid. It was probably a hard time for our parents but they never put it across to us that it was. My mom was always busy. She had three kids and did the books for the mill and still had to make sure the house was kept up, and if someone came for supper she had to make sure that there was enough for everybody—and for anybody else that might show up. She didn't have much to say. She sort of toed the line. I wouldn't want to be a woman in those days, the fifties, if you want to look at it that way.

▷ **Greg, born in 1947**
grew up on the Tsartlip Reserve on Vancouver Island, British Columbia

What did we leave in the 1950s? Rock 'n' roll. Elvis Presley. White bucks. Dancing—it was a lot of fun in those days.

Today we lack discipline. Back in the fifties when you went to school, you went to school regardless whether you wanted to be there or not. There was a dress code. Chewing gum and smoking were out. There's too much leniency in the schools. In the school system today, there's no discipline. There's no respect. There's too much freedom.

▷ **Karen, born in 1949**
grew up in Victoria, British Columbia

The whole way of looking at life was different in the fifties. Technology has not made life easier. Now we are even more aware of the Jones's. I think technology has made life more stressful, more competitive. In the fifties, life was a lot more relaxed.

Stereotypes were strong. This has lessened. When I look at kids today, I realize I was a tremendous risk-taker. I was allowed to fail and therefore to succeed. As a deaf person growing up in the fifties, maybe it was easier. It was not an inclusive environment so you either sank or swam. And sinking meant being sent to an institution.

There was a real sense of trust, an honour system. I was a latchkey kid but we had no key. The door was never locked. And we felt safe. There wasn't the fear of crime that we have today. No question, there was a stronger sense of respect.

In the fifties, education was a privilege, something you had to work for. The family unit was an integral part of life. Now it's very fractured.

On the other hand, I wouldn't want to go back. Kids weren't challenged as they are today.

▷ **Anne, born in 1949 in Winnipeg**
grew up in Calgary, Winnipeg, Vancouver, Victoria and Edmonton

We were just watching a movie with our children who are fourteen and eleven. The movie was *Dead Poets' Society* and it takes place in the fifties in an American private school. As a punishment in the school, one of the boys who is about fifteen or sixteen is paddled with a wooden paddle and really hurt. Our children were shocked by that. My four-teen-year-old son said, "Isn't that against the law? They're not allowed to do that!" And I said, "Well, wait a minute. This was the fifties." He was really struck—excuse the pun.

As you parent today, you explain to your children about what's happening so they can learn. You encourage them to question. Whereas, we were just told what we were, what we would do and what we wouldn't do without any opportunity to participate in that process at all. I think now we allow children to participate and they get the impression that they are human beings and that they are equal to us. They may be younger. They may not know as much about everything, but they are equal human beings.

▷ **Linda C., born in 1949**
grew up in Calgary and Sylvan Lake, Alberta

Family values. It would have been nice if we'd brought more of them into the nineties. They were certainly portrayed on television—maybe it wasn't reality. I think about my own family values and I think for my parents it was really important to play with their kids and to do volunteer community work. My mother was president of the Home and School and president of the Catholic Women's League and my dad was involved in the Lions and town politics. You really felt involved. My mom knew all my friends and my friends' moms knew all of us. So there was never a sense of any worry. We could be out with our friends going hither and yon and it was just a matter of a phone call and everybody was keeping tabs on you. And you knew that. Some of those family and community values—I say community because it really became an extended family—I think kids are missing out on that today.

The role of women has really changed. My dad worked but it seemed to me that my mother was working all the time. She worked outside the home, she worked inside the home. Constantly, constantly working. I think it's good that the roles have changed so that there's more equality.

▷ **Dennis, born in 1949**
grew up in Burnaby, British Columbia

My dad wanted to make sure that I had an education. He had gone as far as grade eight. So I had that push from parents of the Depression and they didn't want that to happen to me. And I know that a lot of the parents of my contemporaries were in the same boat and wanted to make sure that their kids got what was necessary to succeed. And a lot of them have. None of us have gone on to be giants in the world but are quietly contributing to life, primarily on the Lower Mainland. Most of us left. Once we got out of school we headed out. Some went to Ottawa, some to Vancouver Island, some to Quesnel, Prince George, Penticton, Lilloet and I moved to Whitehorse. I and a couple of others have stayed away. I have no desire to move back. It's too big now.

When I look back, I realize we've all done very well. We all had supportive family, mothers and fathers. Some have gone through divorce. Some have different kids from different partners. But most are steady, hardworking members of society. I can't think of anybody who ended up in jail, although when we were teenagers we predicted some of us would.

The fifties were a very positive time. It was a simpler time. It wasn't as crowded. It wasn't as nasty. I think that's the key word here. Nasty. It was a different era. You can't swim in Steel Creek. You can't pull fish out of Burrard Inlet any more and feel that they're edible. You can't go duck hunting any more. It's now a wildlife refuge. There are certain places you can't go to any more because they're blocked off by industrial development. And you can't travel the Port Mann freeway at seventy miles an hour any more. Is it better? I don't think so. Not there. I cry when I look at the skyline of Vancouver today because I remember when it was a simpler skyline. Now you don't see the ocean from Granville and Burrard Streets. You don't see the waterline. You don't see the mountains. That's progress. But is it better? No.

I miss the horse-drawn milk wagon. I remember that coming down the street. I have a memory of being on the trolley car that went from Vancouver to New Westminster before mass transit came in. And walking along that railway that was eventually torn up.

The mid-fifties were interesting and definitely a time of change. As a small kid I didn't realize the kind of change that was coming in.

▷ **Dan, born in 1949**
grew up on a ranch near Lundbreck in southern Alberta

We have lost a sense of community. People change, families change. There was more socializing because we didn't have TV and computers and all of the other outside activities that we do now. We had to interact with other people. I liked the ranch and the community and I spent some of the happiest years of my life there.

The work ethic has changed. Kids today have more peer pressure, social pressure, than I did as a kid in the fifties. We had a lot less than kids nowadays and there's not the same appreciation today for the things that you do get. Most expect to walk away from school and walk into a job that their folks took maybe forty years to get. I think that is the fault of us as parents in some ways. Society and the economy has changed so drastically.

▷ **Bruce, born in 1950**
grew up in Winnipeg, Edmonton and Regina

Divorce was unusual in my experience, and as I recall, there was none in our neighbourhood. In our family, my aunt and her husband divorced, but that was the only one that I was aware of. The reaction in the family was quite mixed. I was still pretty young. My recollection is that some members of the family were absolutely aghast, thinking, "They should have stayed together," and others applauded, saying, "Thank God she got rid of the jerk." Two poles, you might say. Most families stayed together but, as we're now discovering, some stayed together at a horrendous price, not only for the wives but, very often, for the children—and some of the men too. It was not all one way.

A great many young people from the sixties never thought that they were going to live to see thirty. I think many of our generation honestly thought that a nuclear catastrophe was going to wipe us out so everybody lived for the moment. So you had a lot of experimentation with drugs and alternate lifestyles, the whole sexual revolution. You know, you might as well do it all now because you weren't going to live to try it later. I suspect that that came out of the fifties.

It was not the golden era that some people pine for. I get very upset with some people who look back on it through rose-coloured glasses. There were a lot of social problems, and I don't think we were fully aware of them as a kid.

Every generation, I imagine, thinks this, but it seems to me that since the sixties, there's been so much turmoil. And I don't mean that in a negative sense. It's constant change. It started off with social change and now it's technological and economic. Maybe this is my own nostalgia, but it seems that in the fifties there was a certain stability that we've lost. It was probably illusory. Then again I was a kid. You could count on things. You knew that Dad would go to work every morning and he would come home every night. You knew that your favourite program would come on at 4:30 every day. And you knew that Mom would always have meals ready and was always there. And you knew that your best friend would be around to play with. I think there was an element of stability that we could probably use again. However, the stability led to a rigidity and smugness that is probably just as well left in the fifties. I suppose that's the irony. How can you have stability without some rigidity? There was certainly racism. And there's still racism today, although it's probably better that it's out in the open now. We were just so damned smug. Some of it was necessary but in some respects, thank God, it's gone.

I'm very pleased how my life has turned out. It's not what I set out to do or expected but I'm very happy with my life. Certainly I have a job I enjoy thoroughly and a very happy family life. We have two good kids. Married my high school sweetheart. I still tell her that she's the only good thing that happened to me in high school.

▷ **Barry, born in 1952**
 grew up in Saskatoon, Saskatchewan

The fifties were such a terribly simple, almost naive decade. Life was certainly slower and simpler. I wish that were so today—very much so. When you see the old reruns and listen to the music, simple is certainly applicable. The stereotyping was cruel. Dad went to work and Mom stayed home. Dad was boss, Mom was not. Even the television reflected this. It was a male-dominated society. That, thank goodness, is going.

It was a better time to grow up in. It was easier for kids and more fun. Kids played more and were more creative. They were also allowed to grow up more slowly. I work very hard as a parent at getting my children to play. We try very hard to minimize the movie rentals and video games. I don't want my kids to grow up too quickly either. They don't need to be cool or trendy. They just need to be kids. The fifties, I think, supplied this more naturally.

We are, in many respects, a better society today. We are more socially aware and the legacy, I believe, of the fifties and sixties is the special interest groups of today. Unfortunately the drug culture came with it, but for everything you get you give something up, don't you? I miss the simpler times and I firmly believe it was a better time to grow up but I wouldn't want to return. Society carried too much hidden baggage. There were too many areas that needed improving.

▷ **Audrey R., born in 1953**
grew up on a farm near Pelly, Saskatchewan

What I'd like to see return is the sense of community that we had in the fifties. That would be desirable. And the importance that was placed on the family.

But I'm very happy about electricity and running water. We didn't have those in the fifties. I'm happy about the dishwasher and the automatic washer and dryer. I'm happy about the microwave. And very little ironing. That's good. I'm also happy that society, for the most part, accepts women working outside the home.

When I was growing up on the farm, clothes that weren't washed on the washboard were washed in the washing machine that was run by a gas motor. The washing machine and the gas motor were outside. That's where we did the wash. Can't remember what we did in the wintertime. I do remember the clothes horse in the house during a winter washday and it was loaded with clothes to dry. And lines were strung all over the inside of the house. Yes, I'm real happy about electricity.

My kids grew up in the city, and one thing we noticed when we'd go to the farm for a weekend or during vacations, our kids became kids again—wading in the creek, catching frogs, wiener roasts and so on. In the city they had a role to play with their peers, but at Grandma's and Grandpa's farm, they could be kids, just the two girls or with their cousins when we all visited at the same time.

▷ **Bill, born in 1954**
grew up in Rosthern, Saskatchewan, until 1964

I don't think that kids are much richer with the avalanche of media and communications. I don't think I was handicapped as a kid coming from small-town Saskatchewan. Today we're missing the things we did for ourselves and by ourselves.

Awhile ago I got fed up with cable television so I got rid of it. There was just so much tripe on it. We do just fine without it. In the meantime, the kids are voracious readers and doing well with piano and music lessons, activities that far exceed sitting in front of the tube.

There's a lot more distance among family members. Forty years ago there was closeness. Today we're very, very mobile. I was lucky to have family around me. We weren't well off, but we did well. At the time, my parents made an ambitious and bold decision to leave all that behind. Still, I'm very fond of going back. The town has grown, although not a lot. The layout is the same. The tone of the town is the same. It's a quiet place that has an agricultural seasonal rhythm to it. I think of it with nostalgic fondness and affection.